NORMAN FRIEDMAN

THE COLD WAR

ANDRE
DEUTSCH

THIS IS AN ANDRE DEUTSCH BOOK

Design copyright © Carlton Publishing Group 2009
Text copyright © Norman Friedman 2005, 2009

This edition published in 2019 by
Andre Deutsch, a division of the
Carlton Publishing Group
20 Mortimer Street
London
W1T 3JW

A CIP catalogue for this book is available from the British
Library.

ISBN 978 0 233 00571 3

Printed in Dubai.

BELOW American and British
aircraft kept Berlin alive,
delivering not just food but also
coal. Not only did Stalin fail to
starve the city, he actually forced
the Allies to demonstrate that
they would protect it.

CONTENTS

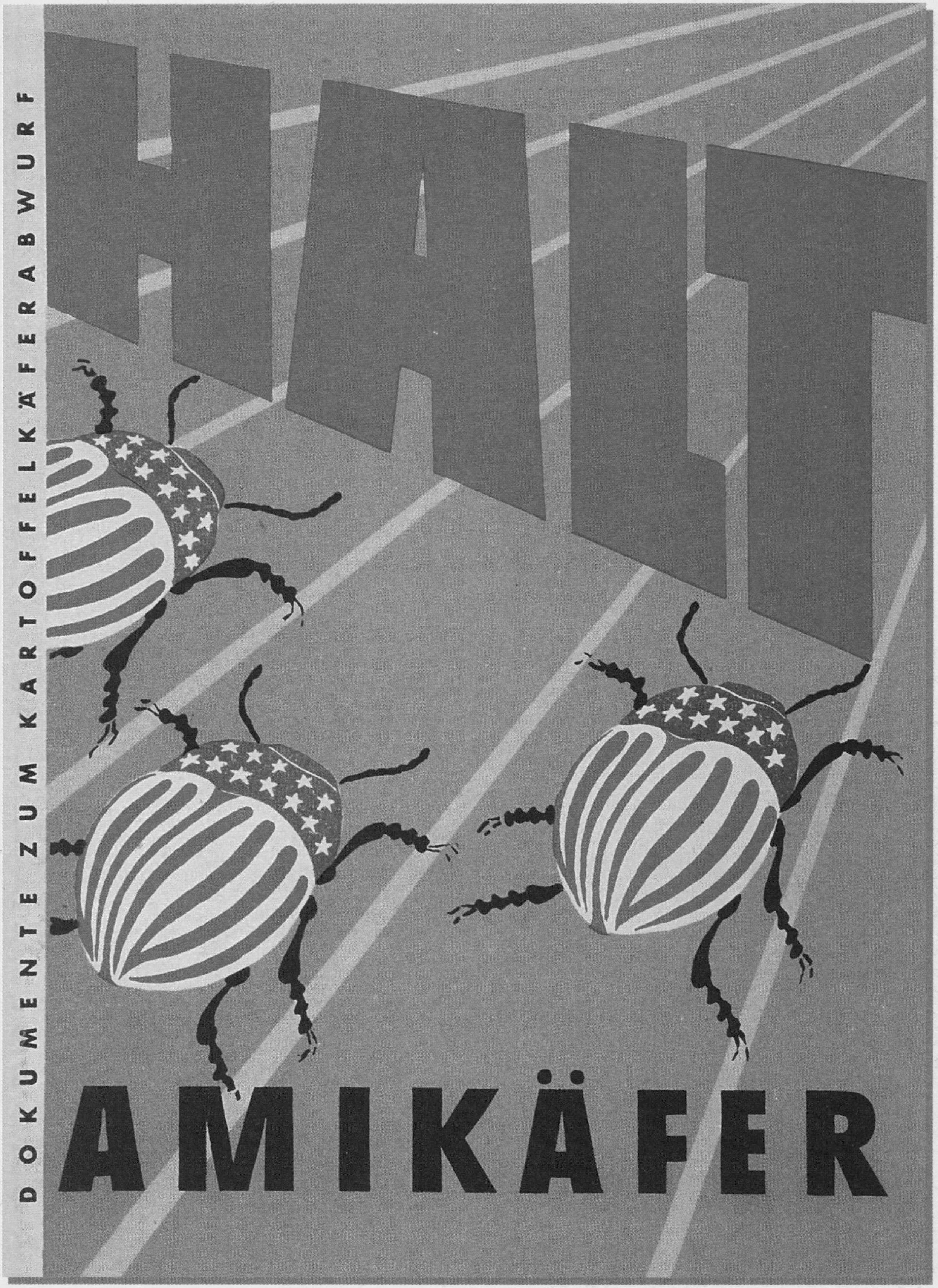
DOKUMENTE ZUM KARTOFFELKÄFERABWURF
HALT
AMIKÄFER

INTRODUCTION

The Cold War shaped our times. To fight it, the West created institutions such as the European Economic Community (since 1993 the European Union) and NATO. Both West and East suffered the consequences of pouring far more money into the military than might otherwise have been the case. Soviet science and technology were overwhelmingly designed to support a vast military machine, the sheer cost of which ultimately sank the country. Western science and technology were often driven by the need to maintain an edge over the Soviet Union, particularly after the Soviets demonstrated their own prowess with *Sputnik*, the first artificial satellite, in 1957. The computers which dominate our world exist because they were needed to fight the Cold War. The missiles created for the Cold War put men into space and revolutionized our world by launching satellites of various kinds. Even the terrorism which currently bedevils international harmony and co-operation can be traced back to tactics each side adopted to weaken the other during the Cold War.

What exactly was the Cold War? One definition would be that it was the West's long struggle to overcome the Soviet attempt to dominate it and the world. Another would be that it was the struggle for control of Europe. Some would see it as World War III, fought out in slow motion and with relatively little fighting. In this context wars like those in Korea and Vietnam were campaigns in the larger Cold War. Many expected the Cold War to turn into a full-scale World War III, but that never happened, largely because both sides feared nuclear war. That both sides so often had the sense to draw back from the brink is probably the most hopeful part of the story.

The roots of the war can be found in the ideology which shaped the Revolution at its formation in 1917. Lenin and his cohorts saw themselves primarily as world revolutionaries; inevitably, the established order would retaliate (such as when Britain, France, the United States and Japan intervened in the Russian Civil War in 1918–20). By the 1930s it seemed that the Soviets felt secure enough to be less hostile to the outside world. Joseph Stalin won power in the Soviet Union partly by arguing that effort should be concentrated on developing "socialism in one country", i.e., in the Soviet Union. It was his defeated rival, Leon Trotsky, who had called for focusing on revolution outside the Soviet Union.

For the West, the beginning of the Cold War was the discovery, after World War II, that Stalin had never abandoned his revolutionary roots; he still wanted to spread his system throughout the world. The policy difference with Trotsky had been no more than a device to gain power; once Stalin was in control, he felt free to change direction. Unlike a Western political party, the Soviet Communist Party followed whatever line he chose.

NORMAN FRIEDMAN

CHAPTER 1

A FAILED PEACE

Initially it seemed to many that the three victorious World War II powers – the United States, the United Kingdom and the Soviet Union – would co-operate to maintain the peace they had bought at so dreadful a cost in blood and money.

As the war was ending in February 1945, the victorious leaders met at Yalta in the Soviet Union. Among other things, Stalin agreed to hold free elections in Poland, which his armies had liberated (and occupied). A few months later the Allied leaders met at Potsdam in newly defeated Germany. Stalin had held the promised elections – but he had crudely rigged them in favour of the Communists, ending any hope of Polish democracy for over 40 years. The Western leaders protested, but they knew that they could not do anything. They still hoped that the Polish elections were an exception, made because Poland was particularly vital to the Soviets; it would be several years before they realized that Stalin's vision of a post-war world did not match theirs.

BELOW In July 1945, the "Big Three" – Churchill, Truman and Stalin – met at Potsdam to work out details of the joint occupation of Germany, the guarantee being that nothing like World War II could happen again. The mood was very optimistic.

OPPOSITE When American and Soviet troops met at the Elbe River in April 1945, Germany was finished – and it seemed that both countries would work together to maintain the peace.

1945

4 FEBRUARY: BIG THREE LEADERS MEET AT YALTA TO CHART THE POSTWAR WORLD; STALIN IS ASKED TO ENTER THE PACIFIC WAR

25 APRIL: UNITED NATIONS FOUNDING CONFERENCE MEETS IN SAN FRANCISCO

8 MAY: GERMANY SURRENDERS, IS OCCUPIED BY US, BRITISH, FRENCH, SOVIET FORCES

17 JULY: BIG THREE LEADERS MEET IN POTSDAM

6 AUGUST: ATOMIC BOMB DROPPED ON HIROSHIMA

8 AUGUST: STALIN ENTERS THE WAR AGAINST JAPAN AS PROMISED

2 SEPTEMBER: JAPAN SURRENDERS

1946

9 FEBRUARY: STALIN'S SPEECH REVIVES PRE-WAR CLAIM THAT COMMUNISM AND CAPITALISM ARE "INCOMPATIBLE" – IN EFFECT, END OF THE WARTIME TRUCE

≡ THE SOVIET BLOC 1945–55

☭ 1947   Communist takeover, with date

◆   Under four-power control

▨   Soviet control zone, 1945–55

LEFT The same paper which reported that "Russia Doesn't Want War" also reported a US guarantee to Iran and Turkey against Russia and a spy scandal.

The victorious powers divided Germany into what they saw as four temporary occupation zones (American, British, French and Soviet) – which turned out to be the long-term focus of the Cold War. Although Berlin, the pre-war capital, lay deep inside the Soviet zone (which became East Germany), it too was divided into four zones, a fact which was later very significant. The powers agreed that elections would be held throughout Germany to form a reunified country. Gradually it became clear that Stalin hoped to cause sufficient chaos in the non-Soviet zones to convince voters there to choose Communists, so that the whole country, the most industrialized in Europe, would fall into his hands. The British and the Americans reluctantly realized that unless they helped rebuild the parts of Germany they occupied, merely feeding the people there would be ruinously expensive. To that end they joined their zones, creating a new currency separate from that in the Soviet zone to the east – and

JOSEPH V. STALIN (1879–1953)

Stalin rose to absolute power in the Soviet Union following Lenin's death in 1924; by 1936 he was in full control, eliminating all potential rivals in a series of staged trials. Although Lenin had created the system of concentration camps, under Stalin millions of people were imprisoned or shot. Millions of others died in famines he caused, particularly in Ukraine. Stalin justified his tyranny on the ground that it was necessary for the crash industrialization ("development in one country") needed for survival.

the beginning of a new country, West Germany. Stalin saw the whole effort as concerted opposition to him. That initially made the French reluctant to join.

In many countries occupied by the Germans, Communists had been very prominent in the resistance and hence enjoyed considerable post-war prestige. Communist parties in France and in Italy were particularly powerful. Maurice Thorez, leader of the French Communists, told Stalin that it might soon be time for them to overthrow the French government. Stalin's own adviser, Ivan Maisky, had told him that the West would not resist as long as his men gained power in apparently democratic fashion. He revived a pre-war policy, the Popular Front, in which Communists were allowed to participate in Western governments (both France – in the 1930s – and Spain – during the Civil War – had had a Popular Front government). Presumably the hope was that a mixed government including Communists could be dominated by the Communist party. In theory, several of the postwar Communist governments of Eastern Europe were Popular Fronts, including minority puppet parties.

☰ SIR WINSTON CHURCHILL (1874–1965)

Churchill led Britain to victory in World War II. As a Cabinet Minister during and after World War I, he was involved in the British intervention against the Communists in the Russian Civil War. His long experience made him quite aware of just how hostile the Soviets could be; he was one of the first to see Stalin as a new Hitler. He saw in Stalin's death a possibility to end the Cold War, and to that end he helped arrange the 1955 summit between President Eisenhower and Khrushchev.

BELOW Stalin rattled his big army, as in this 1947 May Day parade, and he began to talk tough, at least at home, telling Russians in February 1946 that their foreign enemies were still waiting to destroy them.

CHAPTER 2

THE IRON CURTAIN

Only gradually did it dawn on Western leaders that Stalin was hostile. Stalin considered World War II not a disaster, but a great opportunity; it had cleared "imperialism" from Central Europe.

He told a senior Yugoslav Communist, Milovan Djilas, that another war, perhaps in 10 or 20 years, might destroy imperialism altogether. Wherever the Soviet army was in occupation at the end of World War II, Stalin intended to maintain power. By early 1946 Soviet-occupied Poland, Bulgaria and Romania all had Communist governments. Communist guerrillas who had liberated Yugoslavia and Albania retained power in both. Soviet-occupied Hungary still had a semblance of democracy, but the Soviet army held real power. In a speech at Westminster College, Fulton, Missouri in March 1946, Winston Churchill declared that an "iron curtain has descended across the Continent", a metaphor earlier used by the journalist St Vincent Troubridge in October 1945. Stalin was little different from Hitler. Churchill's speech now seems to express perfectly what was happening, but it had a very cold reception at the time.

Until the West saw Stalin's efforts as a grab for power, there was a chance that Popular Front tactics would bring Communists to power outside

LEFT The Czech coup showed other governments that large Communist movements might attack them. The French, in particular, decided to deal with their large Communist Party, but throughout the Cold War it remained influential, and Americans asked whether, in an emergency, it might block supplies going towards a front in Germany. This Slovenian Workers' Movement poster calls for demonstrations in Trieste in 1946.

OPPOSITE In some places East and West collided. Here British military police in Trieste, at that time an international city, arrest an anti-Communist demonstrator during a Communist march in May 1947.

1944
8 SEPTEMBER: COMMUNIST COUP IN BULGARIA

1945
6 MARCH: COMMUNIST REGIME INSTALLED IN ROMANIA

28 JUNE: COMMUNIST "GOVERNMENT OF NATIONAL UNITY" FORMED IN POLAND

4 NOVEMBER: NON-COMMUNIST PARTY WINS HUNGARIAN ELECTION

1946
5 MARCH: WINSTON CHURCHILL DELIVERS THE "IRON CURTAIN" SPEECH

26 MAY: COMMUNISTS WIN PLURALITY IN CZECHOSLOVAKIA; MULTI-PARTY GOVERNMENT

10 NOVEMBER: COMMUNISTS ARE THE LARGEST PARTY IN THE FRENCH ASSEMBLY

1947
19 JANUARY: RIGGED ELECTIONS IN POLAND MAINTAIN COMMUNIST GOVERNMENT

30 MAY: COMMUNIST COUP IN HUNGARY

1948
25 FEBRUARY: COMMUNIST COUP IN CZECHOSLOVAKIA

≡ | JOSIP BROZ TITO (1892–1980)

Tito led the guerrilla army which liberated Yugoslavia from the Nazis, and therefore enjoyed particular and independent prestige within the post-war Communist world. Stalin found this combination intolerable. He ejected Tito from the world Communist movement and ordered him killed. Tito's ejection (or defection) demonstrated that the Cold War was often more about Soviet imperialism than about ideology; he remained Communist but independent of Moscow. His other major achievement, now sadly evident, was to hold together the hostile ethnic groups of his country.

ABOVE For many in Western Europe, the Cold War began in earnest when Communists overthrew the Czech government in February 1948. It was not enough that Czechoslovakia was already friendly with the Soviet Union. This crowd gathered in Prague's Old City Square to hear the new Communist chief Klement Gottwald announce that President Beneš had accepted his demand that 12 ministers resign.

Soviet-occupied Europe, most likely in France or in Italy. However, in 1947 the Soviets rigged the Hungarian election to bring Communists into control. That apparently convinced the French government that France had better resist Stalin; France had been allied to Hungary before World War II. Only pro-Soviet Czechoslovakia, which was not occupied, was still nominally free. In February 1948, however, Stalin ordered a coup there; mere friendliness was not enough. Eastern Europe was now a new Soviet empire. Its population was imprisoned behind a line of barbed wire, watchtowers and minefields – a physical iron curtain. Instead of independent governments, all the new Communist People's Republics were ruled by men chosen – and removed at will – by Moscow.

Finland was the only exception to Stalin's control over the countries his army had defeated or occupied during World War II. In defending their country, the Finns had inflicted eight times the losses on their Soviet invaders that they themselves had suffered, but, without outside military aid, had been compelled to sue for peace. In 1948 the Finnish Communists planned a Czech-like coup, but it was aborted when it became clear that there would be concerted resistance. Finland maintained its neutrality throughout the Cold War.

BELOW The division of Europe ran through two capitals, Berlin (seen here) and Vienna, each divided into four occupation zones, which were not, for the moment, closed off. Vienna (and Austria) would be neutralized in 1955, but Germany was the main running sore throughout the Cold War.

Page 1

CENTRAL INTELLIGENCE GROUP

SOVIET FOREIGN AND MILITARY POLICY

SUMMARY

1. The Soviet Government anticipates an inevitable conflict with the capitalist world. It therefore seeks to increase its relative power by building up its own strength and undermining that of its assumed antagonists.

2. At the same time the Soviet Union needs to avoid such a conflict for an indefinite period. It must therefore avoid provoking a strong reaction by a combination of major powers.

3. In any matter deemed essential to its security, Soviet policy will prove adamant. In other matters it will prove grasping and opportunistic, but flexible in proportion to the degree and nature of the resistance encountered.

4. The Soviet Union will insist on exclusive domination of Europe east of the general line Stettin-Trieste.

5. The Soviet Union will endeavor to extend its predominant influence to include all of Germany and Austria.

6. In the remainder of Europe the Soviet Union will seek to prevent the formation of regional blocs from which it is excluded and to influence national policy through the political activities of local Communists.

7. The Soviet Union desires to include Greece, Turkey, and Iran in its security zone through the establishment of "friendly" governments in those countries. Local factors are favorable toward its designs, but the danger of provoking Great Britain and the United States in combination is a deterrent to overt action.

8. The basic Soviet objective in the Far East is to prevent the use of China, Korea, or Japan as bases of attack on the Soviet Far East by gaining in each of those countries an influence at least equal to that of the United States.

9. The basic Soviet military policy is to maintain armed forces capable of assuring its security and supporting its foreign policy against any possible hostile combination. On the completion of planned demobilization these forces will still number 4,500,000 men.

10. For the time being the Soviets will continue to rely primarily on large masses of ground troops. They have been impressed by Anglo-American strategic air power, however, and will seek to develop fighter defense and long range bomber forces.

Page 2

11. The Soviets will make a maximum effort to develop as quickly as possible such special weapons as guided missiles and the atomic bomb.

12. Further discussion of Soviet foreign policy is contained in Enclosure "A"; of Soviet military policy, in Enclosure "B".

Page 10

ENCLOSURE "B"

SOVIET MILITARY POLICY

1. Soviet military policy derives from that preoccupation with security which is the basis of Soviet foreign policy. (See Enclosure "A", paragraphs 3 and 4a.) On the premise that the peaceful coexistence of Communist and capitalist states is in the long run impossible, and that the U.S.S.R. is in constant peril so long as it remains within a "capitalist encirclement," it is the policy of the Soviet Union to maintain armed forces capable of assuring its security and supporting its foreign policy against any possible combination of foreign powers. The result is an army by far the largest in the world (except the Chinese).

2. Even the populous Soviet Union, however, cannot afford an unlimited diversion of manpower from productive civil pursuits, especially in view of manpower requirements for reconstruction and for the new Five Year Plan. Consequently it has had to adopt a demobilization program which is a compromise between the supposed requirements of security and those of the economy. By September the strength of the armed forces will have been reduced from 12,500,000 to 4,500,000 men.** Further reduction is unlikely.

3. The probable geographical distribution of the total strength indicated will be 1,100,000 in occupied Europe, 650,000 in the Far East, and 2,750,000 in the remainder of the U.S.S.R. The composition will be 3,200,000 (71%) in the ground forces and rear services, 500,000 (11%) in the air forces, 300,000 (7%) in the naval forces, and 500,000 (11%) in the MVD (political security forces). The post-war reorganization includes unification of command in a single Ministry of the Armed Forces having jurisdiction over all forces except the MVD troops, which remain under the Ministry of Internal Affairs.

4. In addition to its own forces, the Soviet Union is assisting and participating in the reconstitution of the armed forces of its satellites in such manner as to insure its effective control of them. While in this its object is primarily political, such forces supplement its own as locally useful auxiliaries.

5. Soviet experience during the war was limited almost exclusively to the employment of large masses of ground troops spearheaded by mobile tank-artillery-infantry teams. Air power was employed chiefly for close ground support. Naval operations were insignificant. The Soviets had only limited experience in amphibious operations, almost none in airborne operations, and none with carrier-based air operations.

6. It appears that for the time being the Soviet Union will continue to rely primarily on large masses of ground troops, but with emphasis on increased mechanization and further development of the tank-artillery-mobile infantry spearhead. The ground support capabilities of the air forces will be maintained.

_____

* As compared with 562,000 in 1933 and 1,000,000 in 1935.

Page 11

At the same time, the Soviets may be expected to give increased attention to the strategic employment of air power, in view of demonstrated Anglo-American capabilities in that regard, and to develop both fighter defense and long range bomber forces.

7. Although there have been indications that the eventual development of a high seas fleet (or fleets) is a Soviet intention, its early accomplishment is prohibited by inexperience, lack of shipbuilding capacity, and the higher priority of other undertakings. Even were these hindrances overcome, geography handicaps the Soviet Union as a naval power, since naval forces on its several coasts would be incapable of mutual support. It is, however, within the capabilities of the Soviet Union to develop considerable submarine, light surface, and short-range amphibious forces.

8. The industrial development, which competes with the armed forces for manpower, is, of course, intended to enhance the overall Soviet war potential. Beyond that, intensive effort will be devoted to the development of special weapons, with particular reference to guided missiles and the atomic bomb. Some reports suggest that the Soviets may already have an atomic bomb of sorts, or at least the capability to produce a large atomic explosion. In any case, a maximum effort will be made to produce a practical bomb in quantity at the earliest possible date.

BELOW Anti-Communist propaganda leaflet *The Truth*, published in 1953 by the West German Volksbund für Frieden und Freiheit (VFF). The cover shows Stalin as a spider with countries snared in his Communist web. Inside, Stalin is shown wanting German unity but at the price of Germans' freedom. See Translations on page 154.

BOTTOM Early Communist propaganda brochure with a moral tale in rhyme for East Berliners: listen to Radio In the American Sector (RIAS) and you'll be on the slippery slope that ends in jail; listen to trustworthy East Berlin Radio (Berliner Rundfunk) and all will go well. See Translations on page 154.

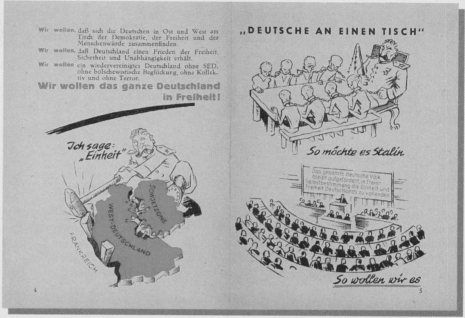

CHAPTER 3

THE TRUMAN DOCTRINE, MARSHALL PLAN, NATO

The US government hoped that the Europeans, led by the British, could handle Stalin largely by themselves.

US involvement might be limited to occupying parts of Germany and Austria. Americans grossly underestimated the damage World War II had done; Western Europe could not revive by itself. Stalin presented a double threat: his massive army might simply invade to install Communist governments, or the millions of hungry, disillusioned Europeans might vote in Stalin's

Communists. Once in, the Communists would never leave peacefully.

In Greece, Communist guerrillas, supported by Marshal Tito's Yugoslavia, were fighting the Greek royalist government backed by the British. In 1947 the British shocked the Americans: they were too badly exhausted to stay in Greece. If the Communists won, the Soviets would gain Greek bases in the Mediterranean, threatening

≡ HARRY S. TRUMAN (1884–1972)

Truman replaced Walter Ulbricht because he accepted the West German opening to the East (Ostpolitik), which the Soviets considered useful. That required greater repression in East Germany; otherwise the population might come to expect freedom. In 1980 Honecker demanded a Czech-style invasion to put down the Polish Solidarity movement. In 1988 he rejected glasnost and perestroika. By the time Mikhail Gorbachev was visiting him for the 40th anniversary of East Germany, a coup to unseat him was already well advanced.

LEFT In 1947, Marshal Tito was the darling of a growing European Communist movement. His picture shared pride of place with Stalin's (centre) and Bulgarian ruler Georgi Dimitrov's (left) at a Bulgarian celebration of the anniversary of the Russian Revolution.

the tanker route from the Middle East to Western Europe.

For 150 years American governments had avoided peacetime entanglements in Europe. President Harry Truman remembered that the last such act of avoidance, after World War I, had probably helped cause World War II. He proclaimed the Truman Doctrine: the United States would help any country faced by Communist attack. American material aid would help keep Greece out of Stalin's hands. The involvement was exactly what Stalin had hoped to avoid. The Soviet leader never forgave Tito for acting on his own. He ordered Tito assassinated and Yugoslavia invaded (neither of which happened). Tito befriended the West. This defection became Stalin's nightmare: the West could accept a Communist government as long as it was not tied to the Soviet Union.

The Americans recognized that Western Europe could never be secure unless its economies were revived. On 5 June 1947 Secretary of State George C. Marshall proposed the European Recovery Program, better known as the Marshall Plan. Aid was conditional on the Europeans developing a US-approved plan. The British were

ABOVE In 1947, it seemed quite possible that Communists might seize power in France and in Italy. Here, a Communist crowd flees French colonial troops in Nice, in December 1947.

THE FOUNDING MEMBERS OF NATO 1949

Founding member

1944
DECEMBER: GREEK CIVIL WAR BREAKS OUT; BRITISH BACK GREEK GOVERNMENT

1947
21 FEBRUARY: BRITISH TELL AMERICANS THEY WILL BE STOPPING THEIR FUNDING OF THE GREEK GOVERNMENT

12 MARCH: TRUMAN ANNOUNCES TRUMAN DOCTRINE

5 JUNE: MARSHALL PROPOSES MARSHALL PLAN

2 JULY: SOVIETS REJECT MARSHALL PLAN AID AND FORCE EASTERN EUROPEANS TO DO LIKEWISE

22 SEPTEMBER: SOVIETS CREATE COMINFORM TO CO-ORDINATE COMMUNIST REGIMES

1948
17 MARCH: TREATY OF BRUSSELS: WESTERN EUROPEAN UNION FORMED

1949
24 AUGUST: NATO TREATY EFFECTIVE WITH ACCESSION OF FRANCE

1955
9 MAY: WEST GERMANY JOINS NATO

14 MAY: WARSAW PACT (COMMUNIST MILITARY ALLIANCE) FORMED

ABOVE The first consignment of sugar under the Marshall Aid Plan arrives at the Royal Victoria Docks in London. John Strachey, the Minister for Food, is there to receive it: (left to right) Mr Strachey, E. M. Holmgreen (representative of Marshall Aid), C. E. Mason (skipper of the *Caribbean Sugar* ship) and Dr W. King (Assistant Agricultural Attaché) watching the unloading.

OPPOSITE The United States rearmed Western Europe to help it stand up to the Soviets. The Western Europeans had the troops, but not the resources to provide them with modern weapons. These American-supplied medium tanks equipped the French Second Hussars Regiment, parading down the Champs Elysées on Bastille Day, 14 July 1954.

the first to welcome aid. US planners saw Western Europe as a single economic unit, and pressed for economic union; the Marshall Plan ultimately led to the current European Union. The Plan touched off the unprecedented post-war revival of Western Europe. It included West Germany, then occupied by the Americans, British and French. About $13 billion was provided in 1948–53. Stalin rejected the Marshall Plan (and ordered the Poles and the Czechs to do likewise). Czech interest showed him that he had insufficient

control over their country; hence the February 1948 coup there. The coup dramatized the threat posed by large Communist parties in the West; the United States provided crucial aid which helped the Christian Democrats win the 1948 Italian elections against Communists backed by Stalin.

No single European country could defend against the huge Soviet machine. Although the traditionally isolationist United States would not initiate a defensive union, it might join a union already formed by the Europeans. Knowing this,

the British Foreign Secretary, Ernest Bevin, initiated the formation of a Western European Union (Britain, France, Belgium, Luxembourg and the Netherlands). Once that had been created, in 1949 the Americans created the North Atlantic Treaty Organization from it (additional members were the United States, Canada, Denmark, Iceland, Italy, Norway and Portugal). The key pledge was that "an attack on one is an attack on all," but initially the main American contribution was plentiful supplies of surplus equipment. To revive European military industry the United States paid for local production of military equipment, such as the first jet fighters to be built in many European countries. The United States also funded much European military research and development, again as a way of reviving vital European industries.

CHAPTER 4

THE BERLIN AIRLIFT

By early 1948 the economy in the zones of Germany occupied by the British and the Americans was reviving; on 18 June they introduced a new currency to fight Stalin's attempt to cause runaway inflation throughout Germany.

Stalin's German Party leader, Wilhelm Pieck, warned that the projected October 1948 elections in Berlin would be disastrous for the Communists unless the Western Allies were ousted from the city. Stalin had leverage: everything consumed in the sectors of Berlin occupied by the Western powers – West Berlin – came either directly from the Soviet zone or by road, rail or canal from the Western-occupied parts of Germany. Stalin decided to show the West Berliners that the Western powers could not protect them. He began to restrict land access to the city; on 23 June 1948 electricity and all supplies from East Germany were cut off. The next day Stalin barred all road, barge and rail traffic from the Western zones. He declared that the Western powers no longer had any rights to administer their zones. West Berliners were offered supplies in East Berlin, on condition that they accepted Soviet authority. Stalin seemed to be willing to risk war; his Berlin blockade was the first serious global crisis of the Cold War.

The Western Allies rejected Stalin's demands. They kept West Berlin alive by supplying it by air. The airlift began on 28 June 1948, when 150 aircraft brought in 400 tons of supplies. By mid-

ABOVE US Medal for Humane Acts, 1949.

ABOVE The Western Allies had one thing Stalin did not reckon with: planes. Stalin realized that the only way to stop them was to shoot them down – and he wanted victory without the war that doing so would have caused.

OPPOSITE The end of the Soviet blockade: a crowd greets the first British convoy to drive through the border checkpoint at Helmstedt on 12 May 1949.

BERLIN AIRLIFT 1948–49

Zones of occupation in Germany
- British
- American
- French
- Soviet

⊕ Western airbase
⇒ Western air corridor
◆ Under four-power control

(inset below)

(Zones economically united from 1948; Federal Republic of Germany from 1949)

(German Democratic Republic from 1949)

BERLIN

Havel Lake used by British Sunderland flying boats

1947
1 JANUARY: BIZONIA FORMED: US AND BRITISH UNIFY THEIR GERMAN OCCUPATION ZONES

1948
MARCH: GEN LUCIUS CLAY, US COMMANDER IN BERLIN, WARNS OF IMPENDING WAR

18 JUNE: WESTERN POWERS INTRODUCE A NEW SINGLE CURRENCY IN THEIR ZONES

24 JUNE: STALIN CLOSES LAND ACCESS TO BERLIN

28 JUNE: AIRLIFT BEGINS

1949
12 MAY: STALIN COMPELLED TO OPEN LAND ACCESS; AIRLIFT SUCCESSFUL

23 MAY: WEST GERMAN STATE PROCLAIMED

30 SEPTEMBER: AIRLIFT OFFICIALLY ENDS AFTER MORE THAN 275,000 FLIGHTS

7 OCTOBER: EAST GERMAN STATE PROCLAIMED

July British and American aircraft were providing 2,750 tons per day. That rose to 4,500 and then to 5,600 tons per day, partly using the new Tegel airport built by the West Berliners. The Soviets ended the blockade on 12 May 1949. About 2.5 million tons were delivered, at a cost of 60 American and British aircrew who died in crashes.

The Berlin airlift showed many in Europe that the West was willing to stand up to Stalin, and it showed Berliners that the West would accept serious risks (like having aircraft shot down *en route*) for their sake. The crisis was so serious that it drove the British and the Americans into their first post-World War II joint military planning, for fear that war might really be imminent. In July 1948 the United States moved B-29 bombers to Britain, the first US bombers based there since World War II. The gesture was particularly significant because the B-29, which had dropped the atomic bombs on Japan in 1945, was considered an atomic bomber. However, those planes sent to Britain were not equipped to drop atomic bombs (as Stalin's spies probably told him).To the Soviets, the airlift demonstrated not only Western resolve, but also Western air power. Unknown to the West, the Soviets concluded that they could not shoot down the aircraft supplying West Berlin. Where cargo-carriers could go, so could bombers; Stalin ordered an urgent programme to develop new air defences for the Soviet Union.

ABOVE American and British aircraft kept Berlin alive, delivering not just food but also coal. Not only did Stalin fail to starve the city, he actually forced the Allies to demonstrate that they would protect it.

LEFT After the Soviets cut off Berlin, everything – even coal, such as the millionth sack being unloaded here – had to come by air.

LEFT Victory for the Allies: the first bus arrives in Berlin from Hanover: "Hurrah! We are still alive."

BELOW Defeat for Stalin: now that the blockade had failed, the Western Allies were able to organize their three zones into a viable West German republic, which was set up a few months after the airlift victory. Here Konrad Adenauer takes office as the first West German Chancellor, in September 1949. As "der Alte", Adenauer served as Chancellor until 1963, setting staunch pro-Western policies for West Germany and refusing to accept the post-war settlement which had given large tracts of formerly German territory to Poland and the Soviet Union. He led West Germany into the European Economic Community, which became the European Union, in the latter as part of a very close relationship with Germany's long-time enemy, France.

"The British Government is determined to remain in Berlin under all circumstances."

„Die britische Regierung ist entschlossen, unter allen Umständen in Berlin zu bleiben."

**Mr. BEVIN, British Foreign Minister
May 20th, 1948   Scarborough**

PSS (B) 7466/10m/5.48

BELOW."Yankee Beetles: Stop!" The front cover
and an inside page from an East German propaganda
leaflet alleging that the Berlin Airlift was a cover for
American airdrops of Colorado beetles to ruin East
German potato crops. "Colorado beetles are smaller
than atom bombs, but they are another American
imperialist weapon against the peace-loving and
hard-working population." See Translations on page 154.

CHAPTER 5

CHINA AND DECOLONIZATION

The Cold War was also fought outside Europe. Japanese victories in World War II largely ejected the Europeans from their Asian empires.

As in Europe, Communists had been heavily involved in resistance efforts, and at the end of the war they tried to seize power in places such as Malaya and Vietnam. European attempts to reoccupy their empires proved difficult, partly because World War II had proven so crippling and partly because the Japanese triumphs had destroyed so much of the prestige on which European power in Asia depended.

The same US government which was so intent on preventing Soviet empire-building in Western Europe tended to support decolonization in Asia. Thus, in 1949 it was American pressure which forced the Dutch to concede independence to Indonesia. It would be several more years before the US position swung more towards supporting what was left of the European empires, but the conflict between the American positions inside and outside Europe would help cause serious turmoil within the Western Alliance.

Another factor was China. While Stalin seized Central Europe, a civil war raged in China. In 1949, Mao Zedong's Communists won the war, to some extent with Soviet help. Partisans of his

SUKARNO (1901–1970)

Sukarno led Indonesia to independence from the Netherlands. Although nominally non-aligned, by 1964 he was so impressed by Communist successes in South Vietnam and in Laos that he thought Communism the wave of the future, and he moved towards an alliance with Mao. He publicly embraced his Communist party (the largest outside a Communist country), and he fought an undeclared war with Malaysia. Failure in that war and American support for South Vietnam encouraged the Indonesian Army to overthrow Sukarno in 1965 to forestall an expected Communist coup.

OPPOSITE The face of the enemy: a wounded terrorist is captured in Malaya. The British enjoyed unusual success in dealing with Communist terrorists, who began their war in Malaya in 1948, and were not considered defeated until 1960. One major advantage was that the terrorists did not enjoy a sanctuary across the border, as the Viet Cong did in Vietnam.

ABOVE India was the first of the great European colonies to become independent. This crowd greeted Lord and Lady Mountbatten as they arrived at the Indian Constituent Assembly to give the Independence Proclamation on 15 August 1947.

1945
AUGUST–SEPTEMBER: JAPANESE SURRENDER, OFTEN TO LOCAL GUERRILLAS

2 SEPTEMBER: HO CHI MINH PROCLAIMS REPUBLIC OF VIETNAM

17 NOVEMBER: SUKARNO PROCLAIMS INDONESIAN REPUBLIC (DUTCH FIGHT HIM)

1947
15 AUGUST: INDIAN INDEPENDENCE PROCLAIMED; FIRST MAJOR EUROPEAN COLONY FREED

1948
16 JUNE: WAR AGAINST BRITISH BREAKS OUT IN MALAYA

1949
1 OCTOBER: MAO ZEDONG PROCLAIMS PEOPLE'S REPUBLIC OF CHINA

1950
15 AUGUST: INDONESIAN REPUBLIC PROCLAIMED AFTER DUTCH WITHDRAWAL

1954
7 MAY: FRENCH DEFEATED AT DIEN BIEN PHU IN VIETNAM

1 NOVEMBER: WAR AGAINST FRENCH BREAKS OUT IN ALGERIA

1955
18 APRIL: NON-ALIGNED MOVEMENT FORMED AT BANDUNG; CHINA A LEADING MEMBER

ABOVE The Communist Việt Minh were one of several independence movements in colonial Asia, but they began to win their war after Mao won in China and provided them with sanctuary (and arms) across the border. This depicts victory over the French at Dien Bien Phu on 7 May 1954.

opponent, Chiang Kai-shek, claimed that the United States had not helped enough, and that at a key moment it had stopped Chiang's armies in the hope of brokering a compromise settlement. Although China had never been a colony, the country had been forced to grant foreign powers such as Britain and Japan (and, to a lesser extent, the United States) humiliating concessions. Mao presented his victory as another form of decolonization. He claimed a kind of senior role among the independence movements and their successor governments. For the moment, Mao could help Communist-led

independence movements in neighbouring countries, such as Vietnam.

In some ways Mao was like Tito, nominally loyal to the world Communist movement, but with the sort of independent prestige Stalin feared and resented. Stalin seems to have been a less than enthusiastic backer; he hoped that Mao would not succeed completely in the civil war he was fighting. Once Mao had won, Stalin's problem was to make sure that he did not suddenly decide to abandon him in favour of the West – which could offer much more help in rebuilding China after the devastation of World War II and civil war.

"Political power grows out of the barrel of a gun."

MAO ZEDONG

≡ MAO ZEDONG (1893–1976)

Zedong led the Chinese Communists to victory in the Chinese Civil War (1946–49), and decided to enter the Korean War largely to cement that victory (anti-Communists would be seen as traitors). He was shocked when the Soviets did not look upon him as Stalin's natural successor. Mao thought China could be developed industrially simply by unleashing the people's political energy. The resulting disasters began with the "Great Leap Forward" (1958–61) and culminated in the Great Cultural Revolution (1966–71).

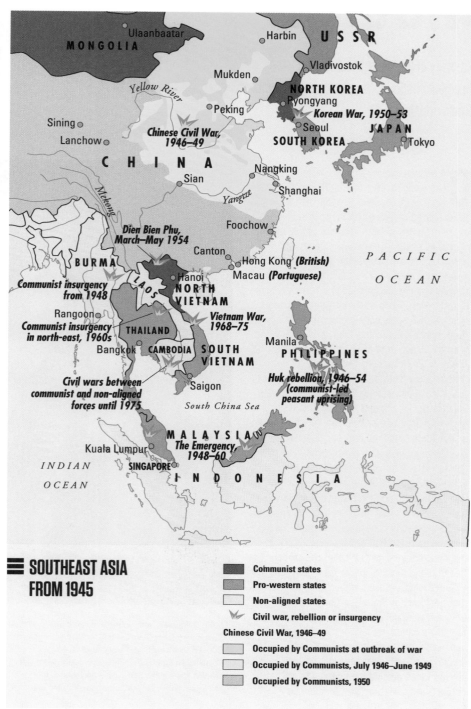

≡ SOUTHEAST ASIA FROM 1945

- Communist states
- Pro-western states
- Non-aligned states
- ⚡ Civil war, rebellion or insurgency

Chinese Civil War, 1946–49
- Occupied by Communists at outbreak of war
- Occupied by Communists, July 1946–June 1949
- Occupied by Communists, 1950

CHAPTER 6

MCCARTHYISM

To many in the West, the Cold War seemed to be a new kind of conflict, in which shadowy, treacherous Communists in their countries helped Stalin attack.

D id treason explain why the United States was doing so little to stop Stalin? Surely he could not have developed his own atomic bomb (tested in August 1949, much earlier than expected) without having traitors supply the necessary plans. There was an element of truth in such ideas; the Soviets had penetrated the US government to some extent, but those charging treason grossly exaggerated what had happened. Unfortunately, much of the crucial evidence of treason (derived by code-breaking) could not be used. Hence the decades-long debates over the two most celebrated cases of the time, the Hiss Trial and the Rosenberg Trial.

Republican Senator Joseph McCarthy found the political opportunity too good to pass up. Beginning with a speech in 1950, he attracted enormous attention by charging that the Truman administration had not only bungled security investigations, it was actively harbouring Communists. Although entirely false, this charge was so sensational that it guaranteed attention. Constantly changing the number of supposed traitors, and without much evidence of any kind, McCarthy gained political prominence. The idea was not new, but McCarthy was a much more magnetic personality than other Republicans who had tried the tactic, and he was much more willing to make irresponsible charges – such as that Secretary of State George C. Marshall was a Communist agent who had "sold out" China a few years earlier. He levelled a similar charge against Secretary of State Dean Acheson, who had made an unfortunate speech in January 1950 placing Korea outside the line of vital US outposts in the Pacific (thus, it might be

ABOVE There really were a few Communist agents in the US government. For years belief in the guilt or innocence of Alger Hiss, a prominent Democrat accused by ex-Communist Whittaker Chambers, was a litmus test for American liberals. Here he is defending himself to a Federal Grand Jury in 1948. In the mid-1990s the release of decoded Soviet cables revealed that he had worked for Soviet naval intelligence, and that the Soviets had decorated him after the Yalta conference in 1945. The cables also showed that the number of such agents was far smaller than the overheated imaginations of the McCarthyists had envisaged.

1946
5 NOVEMBER: JOSEPH MCCARTHY ELECTED TO US SENATE

1947
21 MARCH: LOYALTY INVESTIGATIONS OF US GOVERNMENT EMPLOYEES AUTHORIZED

1948
2 AUGUST: ALGER HISS PUBLICLY ACCUSED OF BEING A COMMUNIST AGENT; HE DENIES IT

1950
21 JANUARY: HISS CONVICTED OF PERJURY BY TEAM LED BY RICHARD NIXON

9 FEBRUARY: MCCARTHY SPEECH TO REPUBLICAN WOMEN IN WHEELING, WEST VIRGINIA, BEGINS HIS RISE TO PROMINENCE

1951
29 MARCH: ROSENBERG "ATOMIC BOMB" SPIES FOUND GUILTY (ARRESTED JULY 1950)

1953
12 OCTOBER: MCCARTHY ACCUSES US ARMY OF TREASON

1954
DECEMBER: MCCARTHY CENSURED BY SENATE

ABOVE Many Americans thought Senator Joseph McCarthy had the answer. Beginning in 1950, he asserted that the government was full of traitors. It took four years for McCarthy to overstep himself, but his technique of charging that treason explained all reverses long outlived him.

BELOW The Soviet test was a colossal shock, because to most Americans all that stood between them and the Soviet hordes was Stalin's fear of the atomic bomb. It was freely admitted that even the Soviets could eventually build their own bomb, but that it might not happen until at least 1953. When the Soviets tested their bomb in 1949, breaking the American monopoly, it seemed inconceivable that they could have done so on their own; surely only spies could have provided what they needed. We now know that spies were essential, but also that the Russians had enormous reserves of scientific talent of their own.

☰ JOSEPH MCCARTHY (1908–1957)

McCarthy adopted his trademark anti-Communism (in which he had previously had no interest) because by 1950 he had so little to show for three years in the Senate (Washington reporters had voted him the worst – most useless – Senator) and he had to face re-election in 1952. He was entirely without conscience or conviction. He is remembered for his blank sheet of paper, which he always claimed listed senior Communists in the US government – but which he never allowed anyone to read.

BELOW McCarthyism worked because Americans knew that Stalin had used Communists throughout Europe to overthrow governments. Many films like this one highlighted the underground war against them.

THE SATURDAY EVENING POST SERIAL THAT JOLTED MILLIONS!

WARNER BROS. BRING IT TO THE SCREEN!

"I WAS A COMMUNIST FOR THE F.B.I." starring FRANK LOVEJOY

imagined, inviting the North Korean attack). Truman administration attempts to curb McCarthy generally failed, particularly as Americans became worried about the Soviet bomb and then about what seemed to be the beginning of a new World War in Korea.

Truman's successor, President Eisenhower, was unwilling to challenge McCarthy directly: he was too popular. McCarthy fell only because he could not restrain himself; in 1954 he attacked the senior US Army leadership (mainly to curry favour for his own junior aide, David Schine, who had been drafted) and he was censured by the Senate.

That did not stop other US politicians from seeking publicity by investigating Communist subversion. For a time it became easy to destroy any reputation simply by charging that a person was – or had been – a Communist or sympathizer. This process is particularly remembered for its effect in Hollywood, where many refused to name Communists with whom they had worked. Those who had abandoned Communism, seeing in it Stalin's tyranny, could only clear themselves by informing on their friends, a horrible mirror of the Communist practice of forcing those in the Party to betray their friends outside. A "blacklist" kept many

writers and producers out of work, except when they adopted aliases. The practice naturally bred corruption: "investigators" could be hired either to clear or to condemn anyone. Overall, the effect of the blacklist was ironic: those who had suffered from it became heroes, whatever their politics and whatever their willingness to follow a Communist line against US interests.

McCarthy's charges were so exaggerated and ultimately so clearly false and self-serving that in effect he made anti-Communism a bad joke to many Americans (though others continued to believe in him). That had major consequences for the Vietnam War.

ABOVE McCarthyism actually predated McCarthy. These Hollywood stars, including Bogart and Lauren Bacall, marched to the Capitol for a hearing on Communist penetration of the Los Angeles film world, on 27 October 1947.

≡ RICHARD M. NIXON (1913–1994)

Nixon was Eisenhower's Vice President and then President in 1969–74. He rose on the wave of anti-Communism which was also exploited by Joseph McCarthy, and his excesses made him an object of hate by liberals. His experience with President Eisenhower gave him unusually good insights into foreign affairs. His unique combination of those insights with impeccable conservative credentials made it possible for him to open relations with Mao's China. He was also too willing to use "dirty tricks" to undermine his political enemies. Revelations of his illegal political operations brought him down in the Watergate scandal.

CHAPTER 7

THE KOREAN WAR

World War II left Korea divided between a Soviet occupation zone in the north and a US zone in the south.

In January 1949 US troops were withdrawn from South Korea. Beginning in 1949, the Communist ruler in the north, Kim Il-sung, asked Stalin to allow him to overrun his rival in the south. Given very limited resources, in January 1950 the American Secretary of State announced that Korea was outside the American defensive line in the Pacific. A few days later Stalin agreed to Kim's request, providing him with the tanks he used to invade South Korea on 25 June 1950.

To many in the West, it seemed that the attack was the opening move in a third World War. The fact that Stalin had allowed his proxy to attack suggested that more moves might follow, for example an East German attack against West Germany. The US government moved in troops

≡ GENERAL DOUGLAS MACARTHUR (1880–1964)

MacArthur, commanding US occupation forces in Japan, became commander in Korea. By turns grossly over- and under-confident, MacArthur argued that once the Chinese entered the war he could not win it unless he could attack China itself. Fired for insubordination (President Truman refused to expand the conflict), MacArthur argued that the Far East (i.e., himself) rather than Europe should be the focus of the Cold War. He sought but failed to get the 1952 Republican Presidential nomination.

LEFT The surprise of the war was the intervention by the Chinese army, which forced American and other UN forces into sudden retreat through a hellish Korean winter in 1950.

BELOW Cigarette pack given by North Koreans to UN POWs.

OPPOSITE Korea was very much a coalition war rather than a US enterprise, partly because so many in the West feared that a Communist victory would encourage Stalin to start World War III. These Argyle and Sutherland Highlanders are advancing in North Korea, in November 1950.

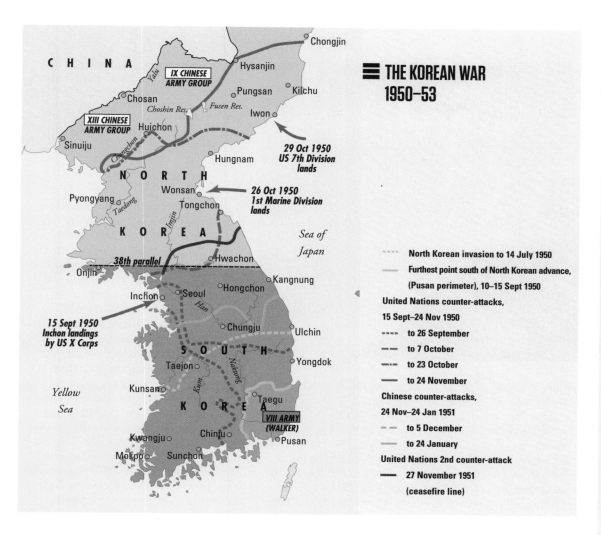

☰ THE KOREAN WAR
1950–53

29 Oct 1950
US 7th Division
lands

26 Oct 1950
1st Marine Division
lands

Sea of
Japan

38th parallel

15 Sept 1950
Inchon landings
by US X Corps

Yellow
Sea

VIII ARMY
(WALKER)

IX CHINESE
ARMY GROUP

XIII CHINESE
ARMY GROUP

- - - - North Korean invasion to 14 July 1950

———— Furthest point south of North Korean advance,
(Pusan perimeter), 10–15 Sept 1950

United Nations counter-attacks,
15 Sept–24 Nov 1950

- - - - to 26 September

— — — to 7 October

—·—· to 23 October

———— to 24 November

Chinese counter-attacks,
24 Nov–24 Jan 1951

— — — to 5 December

———— to 24 January

United Nations 2nd counter-attack

———— 27 November 1951
(ceasefire line)

1949
15 JANUARY: US FORCES
WITHDRAWN FROM
KOREA

SEPTEMBER: KIM IL-SUNG
ASKS STALIN FOR
PERMISSION TO ATTACK
SOUTH KOREA

1950
12 JANUARY: SECRETARY
OF STATE DEAN ACHESON
PLACES KOREA OUTSIDE
VITAL US INTERESTS

17 JANUARY: STALIN
APPROVES INVASION OF
SOUTH KOREA

25 JUNE: NORTH KOREANS
INVADE SOUTH KOREA

15 SEPTEMBER: INCHON
LANDING

1951
2 APRIL: NATO MILITARY
COMMAND FORMED
(SHAPE); EISENHOWER
APPOINTED AS ITS CHIEF,
SACEUR (SUPREME ALLIED
COMMANDER EUROPE)

1952
AUGUST: MAO ASKS
STALIN TO ALLOW HIM TO
SEEK TERMS

1953
5 MARCH: STALIN DIES

27 JULY: ARMISTICE IN
KOREA

LEFT US forces landed at Inchon behind North Korean lines on 15 September 1950. Stalin convinced Mao that by intervening he could stave off the collapse of North Korea and keep the Americans well away from his border. Mao seems to have decided already.

and asked the United Nations to authorize action. The Soviet delegation had earlier walked out in a dispute over whether to recognize Mao as the legitimate ruler of China. In its absence, the UN authorized the use of force – for the only time during the Cold War, so that the war became a United Nations operation, albeit dominated by the United States. Other countries supplying forces were Australia, Belgium, Canada, Colombia,

Ethiopia, France, Greece, the Netherlands, New Zealand, the Philippines, South Africa, Turkey, Thailand and the United Kingdom.

The North Korean offensive stalled outside the South Korean port of Pusan. The United States retained command of the surrounding sea; and in September 1950 its forces landed at Inchon, far behind North Korean lines. The North Korean force collapsed; for a time it seemed that North

Korea itself would succumb. UN forces pushed deep into the country. Then, in November 1950, the Chinese entered the war, reversing the situation. By January 1951 the war had stalled near the original line between the two Koreas. Truce talks began, but the war continued until July 1953. As a measure of the scale of the war, 5.7 million Americans served and 54,246 died. The Chinese deployed more than two-thirds of their army and about half their air force; 148,400 died. Current estimates place the total cost of the war, to combatants and civilians, at 2 million dead.

Because Westerners saw Korea as the first phase of a larger war, the Cold War became a much more military confrontation. The United States expanded its military budget seven-fold specifically to prepare for the big war. Britain rearmed, and the European NATO countries were encouraged to build up their own forces. NATO soon turned to Germany to help defend itself,

THE SOVIET MIG-15 FIGHTER

This was the great surprise of the Korean War. In many ways it was as good as the US F-86 Sabre. It was powered by a copy of a British engine sold in 1946 by a British government still uncertain that it was really at war with the Soviets. The United States offered a huge reward to the first North Korean pilot who would defect with one. Repainted in US colours, this airplane is shown just before its first test flight on 16 October 1953.

first by providing industrial might and then, beginning in 1955, with an army. In response, the Soviets formed their East European satellite countries into another alliance, the Warsaw Pact. The Soviets established the Warsaw Pact in May 1955, comprising Albania, Bulgaria, Czechoslovakia, East Germany (the German Democratic Republic or GDR, also known by its German initials, DDR), Hungary, Poland, Romania and the Soviet Union. The great difference between the two alliances was that NATO was voluntary, each member retaining its own military command structure. The Warsaw Pact was completely subordinate to the Soviets, to the extent that the only command lines ran to its headquarters in Moscow.

ABOVE At times the North Koreans seemed on the verge of winning on land, but they never controlled the sea around Korea, and the US and thus other navies could always support the war ashore. A US Navy Banshee fighter looked for targets near Wonsan, in January 1953.

BELOW Americans saw Korea as a war between American technology and Asian mass manpower, with air strikes like this one as the foremost examples of technological warfare.

BELOW An 8 November 1950 top-secret departmental memo to Dean Rusk, the Assistant US Secretary of State for Far Eastern Affairs, reviewing the possibility of employing the atomic bomb against China. It notes that the "unilateral decision by the United States to use the atomic bomb against China would in all likelihood destroy the unity preserved thus far in the combined UN action in Korea".

TOP SECRET

Office Memorandum • UNITED STATES GOVERNMENT

TO : FE - Mr. Rusk   DATE: November 8, 1950

FROM : FE - Mr. Emmerson

SUBJECT: Use of the Atomic Bomb in China

Bureau of
FAR EASTERN AFFAIRS
NOV 8 - 1950
ASSISTANT SECRETARY
Department of State

If we use the atomic bomb in China it should be done only on the basis of over-riding military considerations. We should presumably have reached a point where the bomb is needed to produce decisive results either unobtainable by conventional warfare or obtainable only through expenditure of vastly greater numbers of men and quantities of materiel.

We should of course defer to a JCS estimate of the military effect of atomic bombing in China. One opinion would seem to be that China offers few suitable A-bomb targets, in view of scattered cities, low degree of industrialisation, and immense area. Targets would presumably be 1) cities, 2) industrial complexes, and 3) concentrations of men and materiel in particular tactical situations. Obviously, the political effects, summarized below, would vary in degree according to the target. A repetition of Hiroshima and Nagasaki would produce the most damaging reaction, bombing of purely industrial military targets the least. Nevertheless, we must consider that, regardless of the fact that military results achieved by atomic bombardment may be identical to those attained by conventional weapons, the effect on world opinion will be vastly different. The A-bomb has the status of a peculiar monster conceived by American cunning and its use by us, in whatever situation, would be exploited to our serious detriment.

Therefore, if a decision to use the A-bomb in China should be reached, we should either:

1) Secure some form of sanction for its use from cooperating members of the UN, or

2) be prepared to accept the political damage in return for the strategic gain.

The following are foreseen as some of the political effects of a decision to use the atomic bomb in China:

1. The Effect on the United States Moral Position.

In view of the history of our attempts to secure international control of atomic energy and of the special place occupied by the atomic bomb as a weapon of mass destruction, the moral position of the United States would be seriously damaged as a result of use of the bomb, without international sanction, against China. Because

TOP SECRET

TOP SECRET

-2-

of the difference in the moral, political, and psychological position occupied by China as opposed to that of the USSR, in the eyes of the world, the effect of using the A-bomb against China would be quite different from that of its use against the Soviet Union.

2. Effect on the UN of a US Decision to Use the A-Bomb.

Unilateral decision by the United States to use the atomic bomb against China would in all likelihood destroy the unity preserved thus far in the combined UN action in Korea. It is probable that U. S. use of the A-bomb would be deplored and denounced by a considerable number of nations who had up to that time supported the action in Korea. The results might therefore be a disintegration of the concept of UN maintenance of world security and a shattering blow to the future development of the UN in the direction indicated by the Uniting for Peace resolution.

3. Effect on the USSR.

Use of the atomic bomb in China would strengthen Soviet propaganda that the United States is bent on initiating general war. Furthermore, should the Soviet Union be prepared to launch a third World War, atomic bombing of China would encourage Soviet participation in war under conditions by which the U.S. moral position would be irreparably damaged while the Soviets would suffer the minimum condemnation.

4. The Effect in Asia.

Should the next atomic bomb be dropped on an Asiatic population, it is easy to foresee the revulsion of feeling which would spread throughout Asia. Fears that we reserve atomic weapons exclusively for Japanese and Chinese would be confirmed, our efforts to win the Asiatics to our side would be cancelled and our influence in non-Communist nations of Asia would deteriorate to an almost non-existent quantity.

5. Use of the A-Bomb Would Commit us Deeper in Asia.

In order to obtain decisive results we should undoubtedly have to engage in atomic warfare on a wide scale. This would involve us deep in Asia and make it difficult, if not impossible, to withdraw in order to fight in another theater of war. On the other hand, should we be unable to achieve decisive results even with atomic bombing of China, the effect upon our world position, particularly as regards Western Europe and countries looking to us for protection against the Soviets, would be disastrous.

FE:JKEmmerson:jam

TOP SECRET

OPPOSITE Top-secret cable from George C. Marshall on behalf of the US Joint Chiefs of Staff to General MacArthur authorizing him to proceed north of the 38th Parallel, which he did on 7 October 1950.

DEPARTMENT OF THE ARMY
STAFF MESSAGE CENTER
OUTGOING CLASSIFIED MESSAGE

TOP SECRET
FLASH

PARAPHRASE NOT REQUIRED

Joint Chiefs of Staff
M. M. Stephens Capt USN
Executive Secretary, JCS

TO: CINCFE (COMMAND) TOKYO JAPAN

NR: JCS 92985   29 SEP 50

From JCS to PERSONAL FOR Genl of the Army Douglas MacArthur, SECDEF sends.

FOR HIS EYES ONLY.

Reference present report of supposed announcement by Eighth Army that ROK Divisions would halt on 38th parallel for regrouping: We want you to feel unhampered tactically and strategically to proceed north of 38th parallel. Announcement above referred to may precipitate embarrassment in UN where evident desire is not to be confronted with necessity of a vote on passage of 38th parallel, rather to find you have found it militarily necessary to do so.

                                    Signed G C Marshall

ORIGIN: JCS

DISTR: GEN VANDENBERG, GEN COLLINS, ADM SHERMAN, GEN MARSHALL

CM OUT 92985   (Sep 50)   DTG: 2920552   dmk
                  TOP SECRET

                                    COPY NO. M-2

THE MAKING OF AN EXACT COPY OF THIS MESSAGE IS FORBIDDEN
                        16—53736-1   51 1454

CHAPTER 8

THE BOMB

There is evidence that Stalin really was thinking of following the Korean attack with an attack in Europe. He may have been deterred by the quick response in Korea, but there was another reason no European war ever broke out: the atomic (and then the hydrogen) bomb.

For the first time, not only people, but also their rulers realized that they might well be destroyed at the outset of a war. Widely publicized civil defence measures only reminded populations on both sides of how devastating the new threat was.

The bomb so outclassed all other weapons that it and its carriers became the main measure of military power. The British developed their own bomb because without one Britain could no longer be considered a major power. By the mid-1950s France, too, was working towards a

NIKITA KHRUSHCHEV (1894–1971)

Khrushchev rose from pipe fitter to senior official by the late 1930s, partly thanks to Stalin's massive purges. After Stalin died, he was unusual among the Soviet hierarchy in retaining a belief in the potential of Communism (the others had become far more cynical). In turning the Soviet military towards missiles and nuclear weapons, he became the last Soviet leader to rein in Soviet military industry (he cancelled programmes to make way for new ones). That was probably the sin for which he was dismissed.

FALLOUT SHELTER

OPPOSITE The mushroom cloud from "Grable", the first nuclear artillery shell, which was part of Operation Upshot-Knothole.

LEFT US fallout shelter capacity poster

ABOVE AND BELOW In the mid-1950s companies in the United States sold fallout shelters like this one, advertised in 1955. To the extent that they had a logic; it was that anyone living far enough from the blast of the bomb (for example, in a suburb) would be threatened only by the radioactive fallout, which would rain down for a few days at most. Cynics asked whether a family which had such a shelter would keep out neighbours who had not prepared one.

1945
16 JULY: FIRST NUCLEAR TEST, ALAMOGORDO

6 AUGUST: FIRST NUCLEAR ATTACK, HIROSHIMA

1946
1 JULY: FIRST PEACETIME ATOMIC TEST, BIKINI ATOLL

1949
29 AUGUST: FIRST SOVIET ATOMIC BOMB TESTED

1950
MAY: DEVELOPMENT OF A US TACTICAL ATOMIC BOMB ORDERED

1952
1 NOVEMBER: FIRST H-BOMB TEST, BY THE US

1954
APRIL: STORAGE OF US NUCLEAR WEAPONS ABROAD (IN BRITAIN AND MOROCCO) APPROVED

14 MAY: TEST OF FIRST US DELIVERABLE H-BOMB

JUNE: STORAGE OF US NUCLEAR WEAPONS IN GERMANY APPROVED

1961
31 OCTOBER: SOVIETS TEST LARGEST H-BOMB IN HISTORY

ABOVE US Family Radiation Measurement Kit

nuclear bomb, for much the same reason.

Worse was to come, however. In the 1950s, first the United States and then the Soviet Union learned to build hydrogen bombs a thousand times more powerful than the original atomic bombs. One bomb could destroy an entire city. Atomic bomb power was measured in thousands of tons (kilotons) of TNT, as in the roughly 20 kilotons of the Hiroshima bomb. Early models could be carried only by large bombers such as a B-29 or B-47, but by the mid-1950s fighter-bombers could deliver their successors. Hydrogen bomb power was measured in millions of tons (megatons); a typical strategic bomb of the 1960s was one to two megatons (later weapons were smaller, as this sort of power was not necessary).

War with such weapons made very little sense. The Soviet leader of the mid-1950s, Nikita Khrushchev, had been raised on the idea that war between Capitalism and Communism was inevitable. When he saw the films of the first Soviet hydrogen bomb test, he could not sleep for days: it seemed that the world was finished. Then he realized that the bomb was an opportunity, not an end: there could be no central war between the two sides, but fighting by Communists for power in the Third World would not risk a nuclear response from the West. He began to ship arms to Third World governments and to revolutionaries. Within the Soviet Union, he paid for a bomb and missile programme by drastically cutting both his conventional forces and the production of their weapons. That made it possible for him to claim, deceptively, that he was disarming, but it also earned him the enmity of the officers he retired and of the industrialists whose plants he realigned. They ousted him, largely in retaliation, in 1964.

BOEING'S GRACEFUL B-47

This was the standard US atomic bomber of the mid-1950s. To fuel it in flight, Boeing developed the jet tanker which was modified to become the first successful commercial jet airliner, the Boeing 707. The rocket-assisted takeoff shown was invented to get the bomber off the ground ahead of an enemy strike: through the 1950s and 1960s the central question was whether one side or the other could save itself by striking first.

ABOVE The atomic bomb dwarfed all previous weapons. The small objects visible on the white circle (actually a shock wave) are real warships, in the "Baker" (underwater) blast of the first post-1945 test series, at Bikini in July 1946.

RIGHT The British Government contributed to the wartime US atomic bomb programme, and soon after World War II decided that it needed the bomb if Britain were to remain a great power. Britain developed three types of long-range bomber, such as the radical Vulcan, shown here, specifically to deliver the weapon.

BELOW US Civil Defence Fallout Radiation Meter

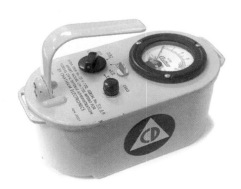

The Hydrogen Bomb

HER MAJESTY'S STATIONERY OFFICE

NINEPENCE NET

The danger from BLAST

Blast is familiar to many of us ; it caused much of the destruction in Hitler's air-raids. As would be expected, the blast from a hydrogen bomb travels farther than that of a high explosive bomb. But it does not strike like a sudden blow ; its action is drawn-out, more like a hurricane.

THE EFFECT ON BUILDINGS

An atomic bomb of the type dropped on Nagasaki, if burst a thousand feet above ground, would level all buildings within half a mile. Buildings between half and three-quarters of a mile away would be damaged beyond repair ; those up to two miles away would suffer severe to moderate damage ; light damage would extend as far as three miles.

The damage from a hydrogen bomb would extend for distances seven or eight times as great. A bomb bursting at ground level is expected to produce a saucer-shaped crater about a mile wide and up to two hundred feet deep, with debris from the crater scattered in a ring about two miles across. The remains of any buildings in this area would be buried by the debris. A ground-burst bomb, however, would not cause damage over such a wide area as one burst high in the air.

With an air burst the damage above ground would extend farther. The blast wave enters through the windows or doors of most buildings and builds up pressure inside. The roof is forced upwards and the walls outwards. Where the blast cannot get in so easily the position is reversed and the building tends to be crushed inwards. Buildings which survive these effects may still be pushed over sideways by the continuing blast wind.

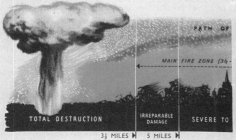

TOTAL DESTRUCTION — IRREPARABLE DAMAGE — SEVERE TO MODERATE DAMAGE

3½ MILES — 5 MILES — 13 MILES

12

PATH OF FALL-OUT

MAIN FIRE ZONE (3½ - 10 MILES)

LIGHT DAMAGE 20-25 MILES

13

RIGHT The front cover and sample pages from a 1963 nuclear attack protection booklet produced for homeowners by the British Government.

CIVIL DEFENCE HANDBOOK No. 10

Advising the Householder on Protection against Nuclear Attack

LONDON: HER MAJESTY'S STATIONERY OFFICE

NINEPENCE NET

6 WHAT TO DO IMMEDIATELY AFTER ATTACK

FIRES

As soon as the blast wave has passed, go round the house and *put out any fires before they take hold*. Turn off the gas and any fuel oil supply, if that has not been done already. Try to make sure that you are safe from any fires which have started nearby.

WATER

If the mains supply is still functioning, you could use the water for fire-fighting. But as soon as possible *turn off the water supply at the stopcock to prevent the possibility of fall-out contaminated water entering the system.*

Remember that when the stopcock has been turned off, water heaters and boilers should also be turned off, or put out. To leave them going might be dangerous.

STOPCOCK

WATER HEATER

BOILER

 Tie up the ball-cock in the W.C. cistern, so that clean water is not used for flushing.

These jobs are so important that they should be done despite the unknown risk from fall-out, but if you have to go outside put on gumboots or stout shoes, a hat or headscarf, coat done up to the neck, and gloves. When you return, take these clothes off and leave them outside the fall-out room in case there is fall-out dust on them.

When you have seen to your own household, help any neighbour in need.

 LISTEN FOR WARNING SIGNALS OF APPROACHING FALL-OUT

20

7 LIFE UNDER FALL-OUT CONDITIONS

THE FIRST DAYS

Once you know that there is danger from fall-out, **TAKE COVER AND DO NOT GO OUTSIDE AGAIN UNTIL YOU ARE TOLD BY WARDENS OR THE POLICE THAT IT IS SAFE TO DO SO.**

Listen for announcements on your radio. It will probably be safe to leave the fall-out room for short periods if visits to other parts of the house are necessary, for example, to obtain further supplies of food or water. *But do not go outside the house.*

This is only a general guide. The amount of fall-out would vary. It would be worst in the middle of the fall-out area, and would grow less and less towards the fringes. Everywhere, the danger from fall-out would grow less with time (see page 6).

You could not tell for yourself how bad fall-out was. This could be done only by people with special instruments, such as members of the civil defence, police and fire services. They would tell you when it was safe for you to come out in the open.

21

CHAPTER 9

EXPLOSIONS IN EUROPE: UPRISINGS IN THE GDR AND POLAND

Stalin died on 5 March 1953. People throughout the Soviet empire hoped the harsh conditions might be relaxed.

When the Soviet government in East Germany demanded that they work harder, East German workers called a general strike. In June as many as 100,000 East Berlin workers rioted; this was the first major outbreak in Eastern Europe. Stalin's heirs decided that their choice was either to stay in East Germany by force or to abandon it, after which they might well be thrown out of the rest of Eastern Europe. They fought: two armoured divisions plus infantry went into East Berlin. Martial law was declared; the riots were suppressed. In East Berlin, 25 demonstrators were killed and another 378 injured; as many as 25,000 may have been arrested throughout East Germany. Of the 109 killed across the country, 41 were Soviet troops shot for refusing to shoot demonstrators. The disaster in East Berlin destroyed Stalin's first heir, his secret police chief, Lavrentiy Beria, who had advocated relaxing rule in East Germany. Among the other consequences were that the Soviets abandoned plans to use East German industry to produce weapons such as submarines for them.

Beria's successor, Nikita Khrushchev, realized that without some relaxation, at least inside the Soviet Union, the country would stagnate. Also, that by attacking Stalin he could destroy his own (Stalinist) political rivals. In February 1956 he denounced Stalin's crimes in a secret speech to a

OPPOSITE Young men throw cobble stones at Soviet T-34 tanks in East Berlin's Leipziger Strasse on 17 June 1953.

RIGHT In June 1953, East Germans rebelled against harsh working conditions and low wages, calling a general strike throughout the country. In East Berlin itself, 100,000 people rioted.

BELOW Berlin police bundle away the first man they shot while trying to break up the riots.

1953
5 MARCH: STALIN DIES

16 JUNE: RIOTING IN EAST BERLIN

27 JUNE: BERIA FALLS AS RESULT OF UPRISING (HE IS SHOT IN DECEMBER)

1954
OCTOBER: KHRUSHCHEV VISITS CHINA ALONE (I.E., BY THIS TIME HE WAS IN POWER)

1955
15 MAY: SOVIETS AND WESTERN POWERS WITHDRAW FROM OCCUPATION OF AUSTRIA

1956
28 JUNE: RIOTS IN POZNAN, POLAND DEMAND LOWER FOOD PRICES AND END OF COMMUNIST RULE

19 OCTOBER: WŁADYSŁAW GOMUŁKA BECOMES POLISH LEADER

ABOVE In 1953, protesters in East Berlin could
march directly into West Berlin via the
Brandenburg Gate. When the Soviets crushed
the rebellion in East Germany, West Berlin
offered a haven – which would remain open
for eight more years.

packed audience at the Twentieth Congress
of the Communist Party. In effect, he admitted
that the Soviet Union had been built on terror,
with Stalin exploiting an illegal "cult of
personality". The symbolic end of Stalinism
was to remove Stalin's body from the tomb
it had shared with Lenin's. However, once
Khrushchev was gone in 1964 quiet attempts
began to resurrect Stalin's memory.

Throughout the Communist world, Stalin's
word had been law. Now that Khrushchev had
replaced Stalin, the new Party line was that no
national leader should rule as a god. That
infuriated Mao, who had a cult of personality of
his own. The same logic suggested that the men
Stalin had installed throughout Eastern Europe
were no longer legitimate. Rioting broke out in
Poznan, Poland, in June 1956. In October the

Polish Communist Party felt emboldened to
replace Stalin's man, Bolesław Bierut, with
Władysław Gomułka. The latter had spent the
war in Poland rather than safe in Moscow,
and Stalin had purged him. Khrushchev rejected
Gomułka. As Stalin's heir, surely it was
for him to choose his puppets throughout
Eastern Europe.

The Poles threatened to use their own army
to fight if the Soviets invaded. Poland was
certainly vital to the Soviets; it was the route
between Russia and the vital army in East
Germany. Khrushchev backed off. The Poles
had gained a small but significant measure of
independence. For the first time, the Soviets
realized that they lacked total control of their
empire. Crucially the new Polish leader
understood his own limits.

RIGHT During the riot at the Poznan trade fair, some of the strikers moved this T-34 tank, flying their free Polish flag, to attack the headquarters of the secret police. Because they did not know how to load the gun, they were unable to fire more than a single shell into the building before moving on. This was violent protest but not full revolution. However, it spread to at least six other Polish cities before it ended.

BELOW Border signs are removed and burned in Potsdamer Platz during the uprising in East Berlin on 17 June 1953.

▤ WŁADYSŁAW GOMUŁKA (1905–1982)

Gomułka led the Polish Communists immediately after World War II, but was dismissed in 1948 on Stalin's orders for his potential independence (he was later imprisoned). The Poles thus considered him their man rather than Moscow's. Brought back in 1956, Gomułka managed a programme of limited liberalization. By 1970 it had exhausted its potential, and he had to reduce wages. He was ousted after rioting, which was the beginning of the cycle leading to the rise of Solidarity.

Befehl

des Militärkommandanten des sowjetischen Sektors von Berlin

Betrifft: Erklärung des Ausnahmezustandes im sowjetischen Sektor von Berlin

Für die Herbeiführung einer festen öffentlichen Ordnung im sowjetischen Sektor von Berlin wird befohlen:

1. Ab 13.00 Uhr des 17. Juni 1953 wird im sowjetischen Sektor von Berlin der Ausnahmezustand verhängt.
2. Alle Demonstrationen, Versammlungen, Kundgebungen und sonstige Menschenansammlungen über 3 Personen werden auf Straßen und Plätzen wie auch in öffentlichen Gebäuden verboten.
3. Jeglicher Verkehr von Fußgängern und der Verkehr von Kraftfahrzeugen und Fahrzeugen wird von 9 Uhr abends bis 5 Uhr morgens verboten.
4. Diejenigen, die gegen diesen Befehl verstoßen, werden nach den Kriegsgesetzen bestraft.

Militärkommandant des sowjetischen Sektors von Berlin

Generalmajor

DIBROWA

Berlin, den 17. Juni 1953.

OPPOSITE Declaration of a State of Emergency on 17 June 1953 by the Military Commander of the Soviet Sector of Berlin, banning demonstrations and public meetings, instituting a curfew, and warning that breaches of this order would be punished according to the martial law. See Translations on page 155.

RIGHT The front cover and inside pages from a special issue of the satirical monthly *Tarantel* (Tarantula), covering the uprising in East Berlin. *Tarantel* was secretly distributed in East Germany from the early 1950s to the early '60s, and its biting anti-soviet humour was legendary. See Translations on page 155.

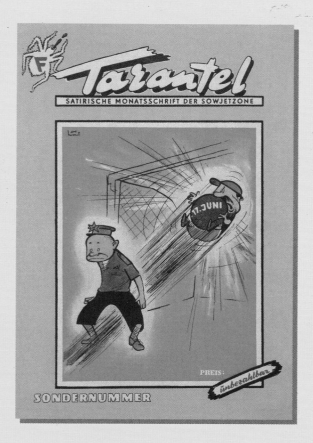

CHAPTER 10

EXPLOSIONS IN EUROPE: HUNGARIAN UPRISING

In July 1956, presumably to forestall a crisis like that in Poland, the Soviets forced the Stalinist ruler of Hungary, Mátyás Rákosi, out of office.

Imre Nagy, a former premier imprisoned by Rákosi, was freed, along with many other political prisoners. The Hungarians were emboldened by the Polish success in bringing Gomułka to power. Massed demonstrators demanded that Nagy be appointed premier. Others called for Soviet troops to leave the country, and in one city the Hungarian secret police were attacked. Street fighting broke out across the country, and in Budapest a massive statue of Stalin, the symbol of Soviet power, was toppled. To calm the situation, the Hungarian Central Committee made Nagy premier, although a Stalinist, Ernő Gerő, retained real power as First Secretary of the Party. He called on the Soviets to crush the unrest, and Soviet tanks fought in Budapest and other Hungarian cities. Poland's Gomułka, who had barely avoided having the Soviets invade his own country, urged the Soviets to withdraw their troops. For a few days it seemed that they were doing so and that the Hungarians had won. Nagy found himself pressing for more and more radical measures: a multi-party system and then a neutralist foreign

☰ IMRE NAGY (1896–1958)

Nagy was a Hungarian Communist initially ejected from government in 1948 (as a possible Titoist) for protesting against forced collectivization of farms. Brought back at Khrushchev's insistence after Stalin's death, he pressed for liberalization, and was expelled again in 1955 for "Titoism". That made him a symbol of Hungarian independence, installed again as premier at popular insistence in 1956. In effect he was swept up in the Hungarian Revolution. Despite a safe conduct, he was arrested by the Soviets and executed after a secret trial.

OPPOSITE The Hungarians were encouraged by what had happened in Poland. Teenagers and women like this one took up arms. The body of a secret policeman lies on the ground.

RIGHT The Hungarians even captured some Soviet tanks like this one, which is flying their flag. This photo was taken during the initial fighting in October, after which the Soviets seemed to be withdrawing their tanks. In fact they were marshalling the force which soon returned to smash the Hungarians.

1956

25 FEBRUARY: KHRUSHCHEV DENOUNCES STALIN AND STALINISM: THE "SECRET SPEECH"

21 OCTOBER: HUNGARIANS DEMAND REMOVAL OF SOVIET TROOPS

23 OCTOBER: DEMONSTRATIONS BEGIN HUNGARIAN REVOLUTION; IMRE NAGY BECOMES PREMIER

28 OCTOBER: OFFICIAL HUNGARIAN DEMANDS FOR REMOVAL OF SOVIET TROOPS

30 OCTOBER: NAGY PROCLAIMS MULTI-PARTY SYSTEM

1 NOVEMBER: NAGY PROCLAIMS NEUTRALIST STANCE

4 NOVEMBER: KHRUSHCHEV SENDS IN HIS TANKS

7 NOVEMBER: SOVIETS GAIN CONTROL OF BUDAPEST AND OTHER CITIES

23 NOVEMBER: SOVIETS KIDNAP NAGY, VIOLATING SAFE-CONDUCT

1958

16 JUNE: NAGY EXECUTED

policy. Khrushchev could tolerate none of this. Negotiations camouflaged a massive build-up of Soviet tanks, which soon subdued Hungary. Nagy and his defence minister, Pál Maléter, were lured from a neutral embassy, arrested, and hanged. About 20,000 Hungarians were killed. Tens of thousands more were arrested.

The Hungarians called for help. However, President Eisenhower told his National Security Council that even rolling the Soviets back from Eastern Europe, which had long been a US goal, would not gain security for Western Europe, because the Soviets would still have nuclear weapons capable of devastating it from Soviet soil. After the failed uprising, some said that the US-sponsored radio stations (Radio Free Europe and Radio Liberty) had falsely promised armed help. Americans involved in the roll-back effort were disgusted by their government's failure to act. In the end, all that the revolutionary Hungarian government could do was open the border to Austria, allowing about 250,000 people to flee to the West.

The lesson seemed to be that resistance to Soviet rule was basically pointless. However, the Soviets drew a less optimistic lesson. They concluded that continued rule in Central Europe required carrots as well as sticks. A quarter of a century later the cost of the carrots would help break the Soviet system. In Hungary itself, so much of the population had clearly sided with the rebels that the government the Soviets installed felt compelled to try to reconcile them. Its slogan became "anyone who is not against us is with us". By the 1980s the Hungarians were more willing than any other government in the Soviet bloc to experiment with innovations such as private enterprise.

MIDDLE The Hungarian Soviet-controlled secret police cowered in terror as people turned their guns on them.

ABOVE Khrushchev ordered in his tanks. For the next three decades, Hungarian governments had to prove their loyalty to Moscow by describing the Hungarian Revolution as a counter-revolutionary plot. The proof that Hungary had emerged from the Soviet Empire was its government's announcement in January 1989 that the events of 1956 would be re-investigated.

MAGYAROK!

A forradalmi ifjak, akik elindították a forradalmat, arra kérnek benneteket, hogy biztosítsátok az elért eredményeket!

Vegyétek fel a munkát, de álljatok készen a harcra is!

Egyetemi Forradalmi Diákbizottság

ENSZ-csapatokat Magyarországra?

Nem volt elég a külföldi csapatokból?

Magyar földön csak magyar katonát!

Vonuljanak ki az orosz csapatok, de helyettük más sem kell!

Küldjön az ENSZ gazdasági segítséget!

EGYETEMI FORRADALMI BIZOTTSÁG

„NAGY IMRÉBEN BIZALMUNK!"

Ez volt a jelszó még kedden, október 23-án.

Ez a bizalom két-három napra megingott, de most erősebb, mint valaha!

Kiderült, hogy Nagy Imre *két napig az ávó foglya volt.* Géppisztolyokkal a háta mögött mondta el első rádióbeszédét.

Legújabb nyilatkozatából kiderült, hogy a statáriumot és a szovjet csapatok beavatkozását nem ő rendelte el. Ez csak a Rákosi—Gerő-féle gazemberek fogták rá, hogy megbuktassák.

Mi tehát hiszünk Nagy Imrének.

De féltve intjük, vigyázzon a nép bizalmára!

Azonnal különítse el magát a hazaárulóktól!

Azonnal takarítsa ki a kormányból a régről ittmaradt szemetet, azokat, akiket joggal vet meg és gyűlöl a nép.

Intézkedjék, hogy a szovjet csapatokat vonják ki az országból!

Intézkedjék, hogy az ávósok ne furakodjanak be az új rendőrségbe!

Nagy Imre helytállását már eddig is sok helyes intézkedés igazolja!

Sürgetve várjuk a többit is. Amilyen mértékben Nagy Imre teljesíti a nép jogos követeléseit, bizalmunk oly mértékben fog benne növekedni.

EGYETEMI FORRADALMI DIÁKBIZOTTSÁG

CHAPTER 11

SPLITS IN THE FACADES

At first the Cold War seemed to be about a unified West facing a unified Communist world, but within a decade both camps were themselves split. In each case the interests of the leading power conflicted with those of the others in its group. In the West, the Americans still rejected what they saw as European colonialism.

In July 1956 the Egyptian dictator Gamal Abdel Nasser seized the Suez Canal, control of which the British and the French regarded as absolutely vital to their economic interests. The French believed that Nasser's support was maintaining a rebellion against them in Algeria. The United States had rejected their claim that parts of Algeria were integral to France and thus came under the NATO pledge of assistance. Nasser had been emboldened by Soviet support, including large arms shipments (which threatened the Israelis). The Israelis agreed to attack Egypt, providing the British and French with a pretext for intervention there in November 1956 (to protect the Canal).

ABOVE The Royal Marines assault Port Said on 5 November 1956, during the Suez Crisis. In the first vertical assault in history, the helicopter-borne troops worked with those in conventional (World War II-style) landing craft. A light fleet carrier was taken over to launch the helicopters.

ABOVE The Sino-Soviet split bit deep. Here Soviet workers demonstrate against Mao. Many in the Soviet Union believed that the Chinese would ultimately invade and destroy their country, bitterly joking that sheer numbers would bury them.

DWIGHT D. EISENHOWER (1890–1969)

He was the first military commander of NATO and then US President (1953–61). Unique among modern American Presidents for his military experience (as Commander in Chief in Europe in 1944–5), he shaped the policy of nuclear deterrence, arguing that nuclear weapons made war in Europe unwinnable, hence pointless. The military side of the Cold War would be fought out in the Third World, often by irregular forces. Understanding that the Cold War would likely last many decades, he resisted buying excessively expensive new weapons, for the war he doubted would ever come.

US intervention saved Nasser. Hopes that the US role would be appreciated throughout the Third World proved futile. Nasser's own prestige soared and his association with the Soviets deepened as they replaced the arms destroyed in the war. The French concluded that the United States was an unreliable ally. By this time war in Europe was unlikely because both sides had so many nuclear weapons; the French could afford to weaken their alliance with the Americans. A decade later France withdrew from the NATO military structure, although remaining a NATO member. Periodically the French tried to persuade the West Germans to do the same.

In the Communist world, Mao Zedong feared that Khrushchev would sacrifice him to avoid nuclear war. The point seemed proven when he failed to support Mao against the United States in the attacks in 1958 against the Nationalist-held islands of Quemoy and Matsu. Khrushchev reneged on a promise to give the Chinese their own atomic bomb, then visited the United States before attending the celebration in 1959 of the tenth anniversary of the People's Republic. Given Mao's growing enmity, in 1960 the Soviets pulled their advisers from China, helping to block Chinese military modernization. Mao loudly derided Khrushchev as too cowardly to support him, or any other Communist facing the West.

The charge was effective because much of Khrushchev's power derived from his position at the head of a "world revolutionary movement". Suddenly Khrushchev badly needed allies like the East European Communist chiefs, and he had to bribe them to stay loyal.

The Soviets began to fear that the Chinese would join forces with the Americans. Shorn of their alliance with the Soviets, they might well assert their old claims to vast lands Russia had taken over during the past three centuries. In the late 1960s the Soviets floated rumours that they were seeking American approval for a pre-emptive attack on Chinese nuclear production facilities as a way of warning the Chinese off. Meanwhile they built a huge army on the Chinese border, at the expense of their forces in Europe. When the Soviets invaded Czechoslovakia in 1968, Mao feared that China might be next. To head that off, in March 1969 he had his troops ambush Soviet troops on Zhenbao (Damansky) Island in the Ussuri River on the Sino-Soviet border. Three years later he welcomed President Richard Nixon to Beijing. Because Soviet forces facing the Chinese could not threaten Europe, in the 1980s NATO countries made a concerted effort to provide the Chinese with the new military technology they needed.

"We are not at war with Egypt. We are in an armed conflict."

ANTHONY EDEN, BRITISH PRIME MINISTER DURING
THE TIME OF THE SUEZ CRISIS

CHAPTER 12

SECRET SERVICES: EAST

With conventional warfare all but ruled out by the Bomb, both sides emphasized espionage and unconventional operations. To the Soviets, a single secret service, ultimately the KGB, was the "sword and shield" of the ruling Communist Party, shielding it from enemies at home, attacking enemies abroad both by stealing their secrets and by conducting special operations.

The KGB led a string of sister services in the Eastern European countries, providing the Soviet government with a second line of control throughout Eastern Europe. These services were generally more closely connected to the KGB than to their own governments. Some of them were also much more paranoid: a sixth of the East German population worked for the Stasi, most of them as informers. The other East European security agencies were the Bulgarian DS, the Czech StB, the Hungarian AVB, the Polish SB and the Romanian DIE. In each case there was also a domestic police agency with its own

intelligence arm. Thus the Soviets had the MVD. In East Germany the foreign arm was the HVA, Stasi being the domestic organization. In Romania the domestic security organization was the Securitate.

At the outset, the Soviets enjoyed the services of traitors, some of them highly placed, who had joined their cause for ideological reasons. Their most spectacular success was to steal most of the information the Soviets then used to build their own atomic bomb. Soviet spies recruited in Britain included H. A. R. ("Kim") Philby of the British MI6 intelligence service. As the MI6

ABOVE KGB badge

≡ H. A. R. ("KIM") PHILBY (1912–1988)

Recruited by the Soviets at Cambridge in 1933, Philby later joined the British foreign intelligence service, MI6. As chief of its anti-Soviet section, he aborted the defection (to Britain) of at least one senior Soviet officer. In 1949 he became MI6 representative to Washington and likely future head of the service. Investigation for this promotion raised questions; the British may have used Philby to feed misinformation back to Moscow. After Burgess and MacLean fled, he was limited by MI6 to part-time work. He escaped to Moscow in 1963.

BELOW Having made excellent use of spies, the Soviets were well aware of their own vulnerabilities. This poster , which is the Soviet version of "Careless Talk Costs Lives", emphasizes that the apparently innocent Soviet civilian might be a foreign military spy (the monocle was a favourite device to indicate a Western plutocrat).

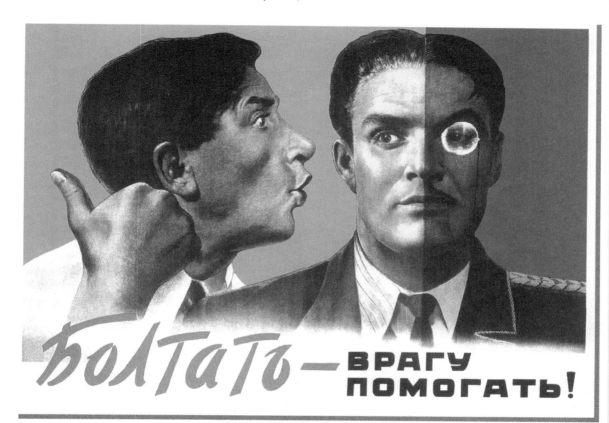

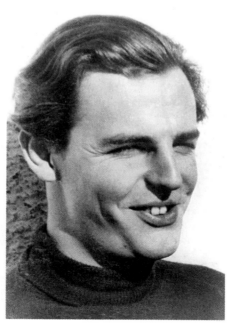

FAR LEFT Guy Burgess fled to Moscow in 1951 with MacLean, apparently on the theory that if questioned MacLean would quickly reveal his espionage. He was a major Soviet agent, and also acted as cut-out for "Kim" Philby.

LEFT Donald MacLean was a senior British diplomat in 1951. Revealed by Anglo-American code-breaking, he and Guy Burgess fled to Moscow, making public the embarrassing existence of Soviet spies at the heart of the British establishment. He had been recruited as early as 1934 while at Oxford.

1917
20 DECEMBER: CHEKA (SOVIET SECRET SERVICE) CREATED

1933
1933–5: "CAMBRIDGE FIVE" RECRUITED: BLUNT, PHILBY, BURGESS, MACLEAN, CAIRNCROSS

1941
AUGUST: JOHN CAIRNCROSS TELLS SOVIETS THE BRITISH ARE DEVELOPING AN ATOMIC BOMB

1943
1943–5: SOVIETS PENETRATE US ATOMIC BOMB PROJECT, GAINING KEY INFORMATION

1945
5 SEPTEMBER: IGOR GOUZENKO DEFECTS

1946
3 FEBRUARY: FIRST PUBLICATION OF GOUZENKO REVELATION OF EXTENT OF SOVIET SPYING IN NORTH AMERICA

1949
"KIM" PHILBY ARRIVES IN WASHINGTON AS MI6 REPRESENTATIVE

1951
25 MAY: GUY BURGESS AND DONALD MACLEAN FLEE ENGLAND

1983
1983–85: TREACHERY BY ALDRICH AMES LEADS SOVIETS TO ELIMINATE MAJOR US SPY RING

1985
20 MAY: JOHN WALKER ARRESTED

BELOW Expert bugging: this carved seal hung in the US Embassy in Moscow from 1945 to 1952, when the State Department found that it transmitted whatever was said near it by modulating radio waves pointed at it from outside. US Ambassador Henry Cabot Lodge displays it and the bugging device at a 1960 United Nations session.

representative in the United States in 1949–50 he was privy to nuclear secrets, probably including the (very small) number of US atomic bombs.

Late in 1945 Igor Gouzenko, a code clerk in the Soviet Ottawa Embassy, defected, revealing the extent of Soviet espionage. Many of the American spies were deactivated for fear of compromising their handlers. Khrushchev's revelations in 1956 about Stalin seem to have ended the era of ideologically motivated spies in the West. The Soviets did, however, continue to enjoy some notable successes. For example, in 1968 James Walker, an American naval code

clerk, walked into their Washington Embassy, with spectacularly bad results for the United States. Code-breaking based on Walker's efforts was credited with ruining several operations in Vietnam, and it probably explains why so many US ballistic missile submarines unexpectedly encountered Soviet warships. More than a decade later Aldrich Ames, a disaffected middle-level CIA officer, single-handedly betrayed numerous American spies in the Soviet Union. Both the Walker and the Ames cases revealed the impotence of US counter-intelligence.

Like their Western rivals, the Soviets also developed intelligence technology. For example,

MARKUS WOLF (1923–1923)

Wolf was the founder and long-time chief of the East German foreign intelligence agency. He was enormously successful in running agents in West Germany, as the West Germans tended to embrace those who had apparently chosen to escape the East. Perhaps his greatest success was inserting Günter Guillaume as Willy Brandt's personal assistant, privy to West German (and often to Western) policy-making. Brandt was Chancellor of West Germany at the time. Wolf retired in 1987, but he was probably involved in the final East German coup.

ABOVE For the CIA, the most destructive Soviet spy may have been Aldrich Ames, who betrayed several very important US spies. He remained undetected for years because the agency had torn itself apart so badly more than a decade earlier in an attempt to find a probably non-existent mole, possibly largely because of the embarrassment felt by senior officers who had never suspected "Kim" Philby when he had worked in Washington from 1949–51. Here Ames is arrested in Washington, on 21 February 1994.

STASI SUSPECT'S "SMELL JAR"

The Stasi was the East German internal security service. Its obsessive desire to know what every East German was thinking led it to force at least 400,000 (of a total population of 16 million) East Germans to inform on their friends and neighbours. To make it easier for its dogs to trail and attack its enemies, the Stasi maintained a library of "smell jars", compiled on the theory that its prospective enemies would sweat recognizably when being interrogated (in the knowledge that they might soon be tortured or imprisoned in the Stasi's concentration camps).

ABOVE LEFT Stasi badge.

OPPOSITE A 19 February 1946 letter from M16's "Kim" Philby to Roger Hollis – then a high-ranking M15 agent, later to be Head of M15 from 1956–65 – regarding Soviet military intelligence defector Igor Gouzenko, codenamed "Corby" or, here, "C".

they learned how to tap into the microwave repeaters used to transmit telephone messages across the United States. When that was discovered in the late 1970s, signs suddenly blossomed all over government offices in Washington, warning of the need to be careful on the telephone.

Perhaps the greatest difference between Soviet and Western intelligence was that the Soviets relied on theirs to copy their enemies' technology: their leaders believed profoundly that Western technology was better. Thus,

when their own scientists told them that the Reagan administration "Star Wars" programme was unworkable, they still demanded a Soviet equivalent: if the Americans said they could do it, surely it could be done. This futile effort helped bankrupt the Soviet Union, and thus helped the Soviets lose the Cold War. The Reagan administration reportedly concocted other secret projects it knew violated laws of physics, hoping that the Soviets would steal the designs and then go broke trying to make them work.

Secret.

[illegible]

In reply, state NUMBER and DATE.

64A

Top Secret & Personal.

19th February 1946.

Dear Hollis,

I attach a hurriedly dictated draft of a memorandum which "C" wishes to give to the Service directors of Intelligence. It needs tidying up in several respects and I would be glad to incorporate in the final version any comments which you may have to make.

Yours sincerely,

H.A.R. Philby

R.H.Hollis, Esq.,
M.I.5.

КОРОЛЕВЕ ВЕЛИКОБРИТАНИИ ЕЛИЗАВЕТЕ 2.
ГОСПОДИНУ МАКМИЛЛАНУ

ГОСПОДИНУ КЕННЕДИ   ГОСПОДИНУ ЭЙЗЕНХАУЭРУ
ГОСПОДИНУ ДЖОНСОНУ   ГОСПОДИНУ НИКСОНУ
ГОСПОДИНУ РАСК   ГОСПОДИНУ ГЕРТЕРУ
ГОСПОДИНУ МАКНАМАРА   ГОСПОДИНУ ГЕЙТСУ
                         ГОСПОДИНУ БРАКЕРУ
                         ГОСПОДИНУ А.ДАЛЛЕСУ

Моя дорогая КОРОЛЕВА!
Мой дорогой ГОСПОДИН ПРЕЗИДЕНТ!
Мои дорогие ГОСПОДА!

В своем первом письме от 19.7.60. я уже сообщал о том, что по-новому осознал свое место в жизни, о своем решении и готовности посвятить себя Делу борьбы за настоящий, правдивый и свободный Мир для Человека. За это дело я буду бороться до конца.

Я прошу Вас считать и меня своим солдатом. Пусть отныне Ваши Вооруженные Силы увеличатся на одного человека.
В моей преданности, твердости, самоотверженности и решительности в борьбе за Ваше /теперь и мое/ Дело - можете не сомневаться.
Вы не раз будете довольны мною, не раз вспомните меня добрым словом. Ваше признание - я завоюю. Для этого не потребуется много времени.
У меня несколько личных просьб.

1. Прошу рассмотреть вопрос о предоставлении мне со временем гражданства США, или Великобритании.
Прошу также присвоить мне по Вашему усмотрению воинское звание армии США. Я имею достаточные знания и опыт, и не только сейчас, но и в будущем могу принести определенную пользу, работая непосредственно в США, о чем очень мечтаю.

2. Прошу Ваших указаний об осторожной, продуманной, конспиративной работе со мной со стороны Ваших работников.

3. В настоящее время я вручаю ряд материалов, собранных за последний год. Прошу Вашего указания об оценке их и об определении положенной суммы за эти труды, т.к. особых накоплений а меня нет, а деньги в будущем потребуются. Положенные мне суммы прошу поместить в один из банков США.

Таковы мои личные просьбы.

Еще раз заверяю Вас о своей безграничной любви и уважении к Вам, к Американскому Народу и ко всем тем, кто находится под Вашим Знаменем. Я верю в Ваше Дело. Готов выполнять любые Ваши приказы. Я жду их.

Остаюсь, всегда Ваш ....

/см.н/об./

14.8.60.
9.4.61.

69

CHAPTER 13

SECRET SERVICES: WEST

Unlike the Soviets, Western countries generally separated foreign intelligence services from domestic (defensive) ones. Code-breaking agencies, which were probably much more important in Britain and in the United States, were also separate.

The British services, MI5 (domestic) and MI6 (foreign), were both set up before World War I. The code-breaking organization, GCHQ, was a product of that war. The United States created its first unified intelligence service, the Office of Strategic Services (OSS), during World War II, with much input from MI6. The domestic agency, the FBI, already existed, a product of the "Red Scare" immediately after World War I. OSS was shut down after World War II, but in 1947 a new Central Intelligence Agency (CIA) was created. The US code-breaking agency, NSA, was created

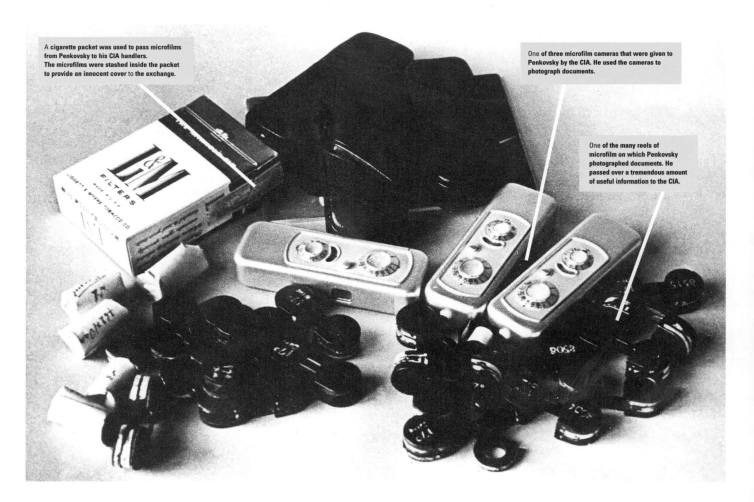

A cigarette packet was used to pass microfilms from Penkovsky to his CIA handlers. The microfilms were stashed inside the packet to provide an innocent cover to the exchange.

One of three microfilm cameras that were given to Penkovsky by the CIA. He used the cameras to photograph documents.

One of the many reels of microfilm on which Penkovsky photographed documents. He passed over a tremendous amount of useful information to the CIA.

OPPOSITE A spy's equipment, as provided to Col. Oleg Penkovskiy. He provided both details of current weapons and the texts of top secret military magazines. This explanation of Soviet thinking of the time could never have been obtained by aircraft or by satellites.

LEFT Photographs could never provide enough insight, though, so the West tried again and again to tap into Soviet communications. This tunnel into the East Berlin telephone system was an early attempt. It was betrayed by the Soviet double-agent George Blake.

at the same time. Other Western countries, such as France, generally had similar organizations.

During the Cold War, the West found it difficult to maintain spies, partly because the closed Soviet society was very good at catching them. In the wake of disastrous penetrations such as "Kim" Philby, both the CIA and MI6 spent much of their time trying to make sure that they were not still being penetrated. The CIA's mole hunt was closed down because it was so destructive. Then counter-espionage was virtually abandoned, with the result that Aldrich Ames could operate unhindered. Even so, there were some striking successes. Soviet society was so badly distorted that senior officers such as Colonel Oleg Penkovsky of Soviet military intelligence offered their services from time to time. Penkovsky's insights into Soviet rocket tactics were vital in

OLEG V. PENKOVSKY (1919–1963)

A senior military intelligence officer, he approached the British (after the Americans rejected him). Penkovsky was responsible for scientific intelligence, which the Soviets often used as the basis for industrial programmes. To see what was needed, he was made privy to many of the advanced Soviet military programmes. His insights were particularly important during the Cuban Missile Crisis. Penkovsky also provided copies of the Soviet military magazines describing Khrushchev's new nuclear-oriented strategy – which he considered so abhorrent that he turned spy. Penkovsky was tried and executed for espionage in 1963.

1943
NOVEMBER: FIRST INTERCEPTS OF VENONA TRAFFIC

1949
10 MAY: FIRST RECORDED OVERFLIGHT OF SOVIET UNION BY US AIR FORCE, TO FIND SUPPOSED BOMBER BASES

1954
FBI RECRUITS MORRIS CHILDS

1955
FEBRUARY: US AND BRITAIN TAP SOVIET MILITARY TELEPHONE SYSTEM IN BERLIN

4 AUGUST: FIRST FLIGHT OF U-2

1956
2 JULY: FIRST U-2 MISSION OVER THE SOVIET UNION

1960
OLEG PENKOVSKY OFFERS HIS SERVICES TO CIA

1 MAY: GARY POWERS SHOT DOWN IN U-2; PARIS SUMMIT CONFERENCE WRECKED

12 AUGUST: FIRST PHOTOGRAPHS RECOVERED FROM RECONNAISSANCE SATELLITE

1963
11 MAY: PENKOVSKY CONVICTED AND SENTENCED TO DEATH

1970
EARLY 1970S: US TAPS SOVIET UNDERWATER CABLE USED BY PACIFIC FLEET

"I was a pilot flying an airplane and it just so happened that where I was flying made what I was doing spying."

FRANCIS GARY POWERS, U-2 PILOT WHO WAS
CAPTURED BY THE SOVIETS IN 1960.

OPPOSITE The U-2 produced amazing results. This picture was taken by a U-2 and shows the pad at Baikonur used to launch the Sputniks and prototype SS-6 intercontinental missiles.

BELOW The Soviets were so good at security that it was almost impossible to penetrate their society. President Eisenhower approved the alternative: fly over the Iron Curtain instead of trying to get through it, using this radical high-flying aircraft, the U-2.

FRANCIS GARY POWERS (1929–1977)

Powers flew the U-2 shot down by the Soviets on May Day 1960. He survived to be placed on trial in Moscow. He was sentenced to three years of prison and seven years of hard labour, but on 10 February 1962 he was exchanged for "Rudolf Abel" (actually KGB Col. Vilyam Fisher) in Potsdam. He served as a test pilot for Lockheed, which built the U-2, in 1963–70 and later died in a helicopter accident, while a radio traffic-reporter.

understanding what was happening during the Cuban Missile Crisis, but he was caught and executed soon after.

Perhaps the least-known but most striking US success was that of Morris Childs ("Solo"). In 1954 the FBI turned Childs, the badly disaffected number-two man in the US Communist Party. Because they acted as though each country's Communist party was that country's future government, the Soviets treated Childs as they would a foreign minister, making him privy to their policy decisions. Childs became personally friendly with the senior Chinese leadership, so the Soviets used him as a go-between in attempts to patch up the Sino-Soviet split. Unfortunately no one at the CIA could believe that the FBI could produce an agent this good, so it was some considerable time before Childs's remarkable material was used – after which it was eagerly devoured in Washington.

Given very limited ability to penetrate the closed Soviet society, the West concentrated on developing some remarkable intelligence-gathering systems, beginning with high-altitude aircraft such as the U-2, and then following up with large numbers of satellites of various types. In this it helped that the West had a much better industrial base. Much effort also went into code-breaking, although it is still difficult to say how successfully (the Soviets were good at code security). One success is known: Venona. During World War II the Soviets had slipped in the way they protected communications with their agents, and Venona was the decades-long attempt to break messages this compromised. It revealed many of the Soviet agents who were caught in the 1940s and early 1950s, such as the Rosenbergs and Alger Hiss. Ironically, the Soviets were tipped off to the early successes of the Venona project by their own agent within the US code-breaking organization (and by Philby); they were presumably less aware of later successes.

CHAPTER 14

SPUTNIK AND THE MISSILE AGE

Until 1957 Westerners generally saw the Soviet Union as the country capable of fielding a mass army (the old "Russian steamroller") with tens of thousands of tanks, but not of developing sophisticated aircraft and electronics.

This image had been shaken only slightly by the sudden appearance in Korea of the MiG-15 jet, which outperformed existing Western fighters. On 4 October 1957, however, the Russians launched *Sputnik*, the first artificial earth satellite. American attempts to put into orbit Explorer, a much smaller satellite, failed dramatically as rocket after rocket exploded on the launch pad. In Europe, the NATO allies began to wonder whether the American military technology on which they were relying to defend themselves was really as superior as they had imagined. The small sphere beeping as it passed around the earth seemed to be mocking the West.

Sputnik was the beginning of a scientific race, mainly a space race, which culminated in the American moon landing a little more than a decade later. *Sputnik* itself was not, of course, a weapon, but the rocket which launched it was a modified intercontinental ballistic missile (ICBM). In effect the *Sputnik* success proved that the missile worked. Up to that time, bombs, however horrific, had been delivered by bombers, and one might imagine a defence against them. It seemed, however, that a missile could not be shot down; suddenly the Soviets had the ultimate weapon in the combination of long-range missile and hydrogen bomb.

Once *Sputnik* had been launched, Americans had the sense that they were on the wrong side of a technological revolution. John F. Kennedy exploited this sense very effectively during the

LEFT Yuri Gagarin became the first man in space on 12 April 1961, orbiting the earth before landing in Soviet desert.

1960 election, charging that the outgoing Eisenhower administration had allowed a missile gap to open between the two superpowers. The reality was different. Even in 1957 the United States had longer-range missiles, but Eisenhower had banned the use of military ones to launch the first (scientific) earth satellite.

Given the shock of *Sputnik*, the Eisenhower administration scrambled to find some way to give the European allies back their sense of security. One idea it hit upon was to give them shorter-range (intermediate-range) missiles – which were placed in Italy, Turkey and the United Kingdom. Until American ICBMs were operational, these weapons would offer a missile

Слушай, страна,
Мечта людей зовет!
Сегодня твой народ
Ликует и поет.

ВСЯ ВЛАСТЬ СОВѢТАМЪ!

ABOVE The Soviets saw their space exploits as proof that their system was winning. This poster makes the connection between the parade and the rocket to the moon explicit. Such pride made it worse when the Soviet moon programme collapsed.

1957
26 AUGUST: SOVIETS LAUNCH WORLD'S FIRST ICBM

4 OCTOBER: SOVIETS LAUNCH *SPUTNIK*

3 NOVEMBER: SOVIETS LAUNCH FIRST LIVING THING INTO SPACE, "DOG LAIKA"

1958
31 JANUARY: FIRST SUCCESSFUL US SATELLITE LAUNCH

1961
12 APRIL: YURI GAGARIN BECOMES FIRST MAN TO ORBIT THE EARTH

5 MAY: ALAN SHEPARD BECOMES FIRST US MAN IN SPACE (SUB-ORBITAL MISSION)

25 MAY: PRESIDENT KENNEDY ANNOUNCES GOAL OF PLACING A MAN ON THE MOON WITHIN THE DECADE

1963
26 JULY: FIRST COMMUNICATIONS SATELLITE IN ORBIT

1969
21 FEBRUARY: FAILURE OF MASSIVE SOVIET N-1 ROCKET DOOMS SOVIET MOON EFFORT

20 JULY: US ASTRONAUTS LAND ON THE MOON

threat against the Soviet Union; but Eisenhower already knew that American bombers probably could penetrate Soviet air defences, so the missiles were more a matter of reassurance than of necessity. As it happened, the first US ICBMs became operational in September 1959. The shorter-range missiles became operational, in greater numbers, at about the same time.

The great irony was that, even some years later, with ICBMs rolling off US production lines, the Soviets still could not build ICBMs in any numbers, probably because they found it difficult to produce precise enough parts (shorter-range missiles were much less of a problem). The shorter-range weapons were a problem for Europeans but not for Americans — until and unless Khrushchev found some way of stationing such weapons closer to the United States.

WERNHER VON BRAUN (1912–1977)

He began the era of long-range ballistic missiles by convincing the German army to develop them – to further his own ambition, he said, to put men into space. His wartime V-2 inspired the postwar ICBMs. At war's end von Braun surrendered to the US Army, for which he developed such missiles as Redstone (which launched the first US satellite). The Air Force having taken responsibility for longer-range missiles, von Braun moved to the new civilian NASA agency, for which he developed the Saturn rocket which put Americans on the moon.

ABOVE By launching *Sputnik*, the Soviets showed that they were the equals of the West in high technology. To the more sophisticated, they also demonstrated that they had the world's first intercontinental ballistic missile, because that was what it took to orbit the satellite.

THE US ICBM

The rocket that could orbit a big satellite, could also carry an H-bomb from the Soviet Union to the United States, or vice versa. The Intercontinental Ballistic Missile (ICBM) typically could fly 5,000–10,000 miles (8,000–16,000 km); by the 1980s some such missiles could carry several warheads, placing each of them within 150 yards (137 m) of its target. This Atlas, the first successful US ICBM, is shown in 1958.

"America has tossed its cap over
the wall of space."

JOHN F. KENNEDY

OPPOSITE AND BELOW UK Joint Intelligence Committee
(JIC) Top Secret January 1968 report on likely employment
of Soviet forces in the event of war up to the end of 1972,
including maps showing Soviet strategic surface-to-
surface missile deployment areas and ranges.

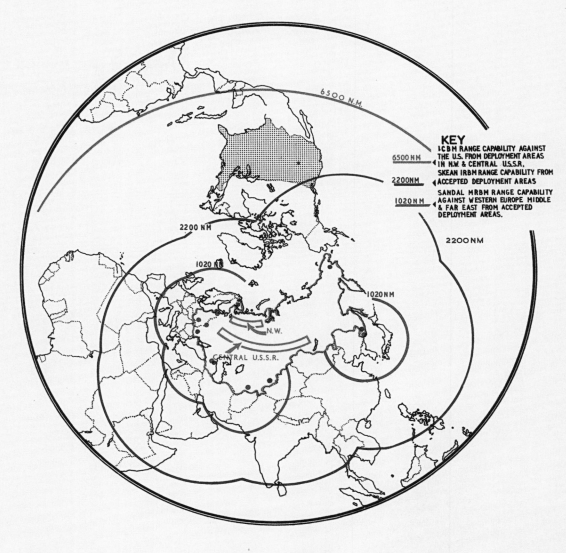

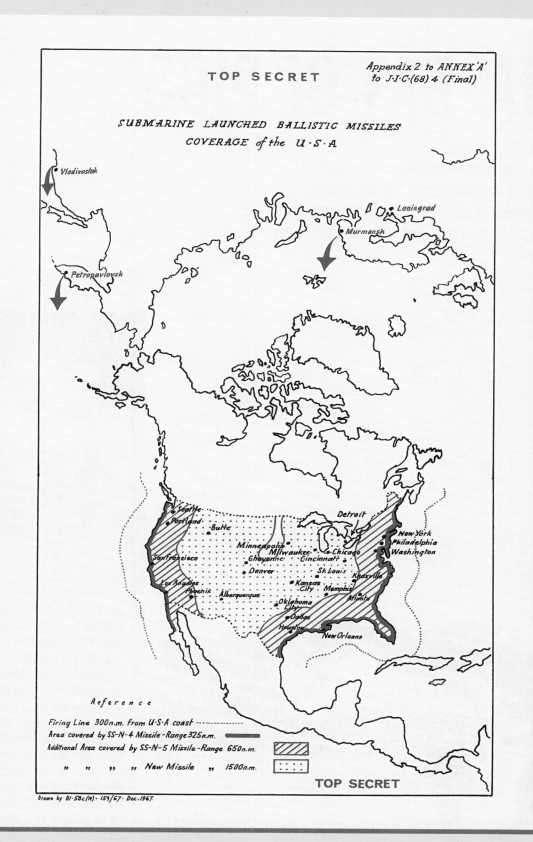

CHAPTER 15

CUBA: BAY OF PIGS

**Two years after *Sputnik*, Americans suffered another shock.
Fidel Castro overthrew the Cuban dictator, Fulgencio Batista.
Initially few mourned Batista, but gradually it became clear that
Castro was intent on creating a new Communist state only 90 miles
(145 km) from Florida.**

During the 1960 election, John F. Kennedy charged that the Eisenhower administration (against whose Vice President, Richard Nixon, he was running) had done nothing about Cuba. The US press praised Nixon, who was usually considered a virulent anti-Communist, for his restraint in opposing an invasion. Few knew that Nixon was silent because in March 1960 his administration had authorized planning the invasion Kennedy was demanding. Kennedy inherited the plan. The Eisenhower administration had used exiles recruited and backed by the CIA to overthrow the left-leaning Guatemalan government in 1954, and it planned to do much the same thing again.

Eisenhower had planned to use regular American forces to back up the exiles, but Kennedy feared that to do so would be to admit American involvement (Eishenhower later told him that it did not matter: any attempt to overthrow Castro would be seen as American). The plan was to land 1,500 Cubans. The landing place was originally Trinidad, near the Escambray Mountains, into which the attackers could fade in the event of some disaster. Under Kennedy the landing place was shifted to the

FIDEL CASTRO (1926–2016)

Castro led a guerrilla army to victory in Cuba in 1959 after a six-year campaign. Once in power, he used resentment of Americans (who owned much of Cuban industry) as a way of maintaining it without allowing any sort of democracy. He tried to spark further Communist rebellions, first in Latin America and then in Africa. He relied heavily on the Soviets, and felt betrayed when Khrushchev withdrew his missiles without bothering to consult him. His revolutionary activity in Africa may have been partly an attempt to make it impossible for the Soviets to sell him out during the era of détente.

OPPOSITE In this photograph taken from the newspaper Revolución, large artillery pieces are shown firing on Cuban rebels as they invade a beachhead in Cuba. It was reported that many Cuban rebels were taken prisoner in the ill-fated invasion, as the choice of beach left them no way to melt into the hills to escape the Cuban army.

LEFT To deal with Castro, the United States recruited an army of Cuban exiles, which was trained in Central America.

BELOW Defeated rebels are marched off to prison. Many Cuban émigrés in the United States blamed President Kennedy personally for the failure at the Bay of Pigs, because he was individually responsible for cancelling crucial air support. Nor was it ever clear why the landing site was moved to the Bay of Pigs, from which the rebels could not have escaped overland into the Cuban mountains.

1959
1 JANUARY: CASTRO PROCLAIMS VICTORY

1960
11 JANUARY: US FORMALLY PROTESTS CUBAN SEIZURES OF US PROPERTY

4 FEBRUARY: CASTRO NEGOTIATES TRADE AGREEMENTS WITH THE SOVIETS, FIRST INDICATION OF HIS COMMUNIST LEANINGS

8 JULY: UNITED STATES SUSPENDS THE CUBAN SUGAR QUOTA

16 AUGUST: FIRST US ASSASSINATION PLOT AGAINST CASTRO

1961
20 JANUARY: KENNEDY INAUGURATED AS PRESIDENT

12 APRIL: KENNEDY ORDERS US FORCES NOT TO BECOME INVOLVED, CUTS AIR SUPPORT

14 APRIL: INITIAL AIR STRIKES IN SUPPORT OF THE LANDING

17 APRIL: LANDING AT BAY OF PIGS; INSURGENTS DEFEATED

13 JUNE: KENNEDY ORDERS OTHER MEASURES TO DEAL WITH CASTRO

≡ JOHN F. KENNEDY (1917–1963)

Charismatic and glamorous, he created an administration of unusual intellectual power. It included many of the new generation of strategists specially concerned with how to fight and survive in a nuclear world; Kennedy's special interest in counter-insurgency stemmed from his belief that the Soviets had adopted Third World revolution as a way to fight the Cold War without risking nuclear confrontation. As heir to the World War II leadership generation, Kennedy seems to have felt a special need to prove his mettle.

Bay of Pigs, further west. Why is not clear. The 17 April 1961 attack failed disastrously, partly because Kennedy cancelled air support after the first strikes (landing in Florida, the pilots were unable to convince anyone that they were not working for the US government). Nor did the landing touch off the expected uprising among the Cubans, and there was no nearby refuge into which the attackers could withdraw to begin guerrilla warfare. US naval forces waiting offshore to support the landing were ordered not to intervene, and the Cubans smashed the exile force. Kennedy's role in the fiasco convinced Khrushchev that he lacked backbone.

Having failed to overthrow Castro, the United States imposed a trade embargo which solidified Castro's existing ties with the Soviets. Khrushchev gained a potential base only 90 miles (145 km) from the United States. President Kennedy was left more determined than ever to prove that he could stand up to the Communists. Just before Kennedy's inauguration, Khrushchev had given a speech proclaiming his support for what he called "wars of national liberation."

Kennedy saw it as an announcement that Khrushchev's new policy would be to attack the West in the Third World. For example, his Joint Chiefs of Staff thought that the Soviets were trying to seize the former Belgian Congo in Central Africa. In Kennedy's view, the most important role for the United States would be to squelch such rebellions, or, better, to adopt policies which would make them unnecessary. The failure at the Bay of Pigs seemed irrelevant; it was time to build American forces, particularly special forces, to take on the guerrillas Khrushchev had just announced he would support.

Castro, too, had proclaimed a mission of liberation, which seemed to be directed at Latin America, traditionally a US sphere of influence. Here Kennedy hoped to foment a social revolution which would make it unnecessary to use force: using the Alliance for Progress, envisaged as a Marshall Plan for Latin America. Meanwhile, many blamed the new President for the failure at the Bay of Pigs, and he certainly became determined to overthrow Castro, sponsoring a string of failed assassination plots.

ABOVE Political disaster: few believed the Bay of Pigs had been anything but a US operation, despite President Kennedy's attempts to distance himself from it. Indian Communists march to the US embassy in New Delhi on 21 April 1961.

RIGHT Surrounding one of the landing craft, Cubans celebrate their victory over the US-backed invaders at the Bay of Pigs.

CHAPTER 16
THE BERLIN WALL

The German capital, 110 miles (175 km) inside East Germany, was divided between Allied (West) and Soviet (East) zones, but the line between the two was open.

By 1961 skilled East Germans were fleeing so quickly that a Russian joker suggested that soon only the hated ruler of the country, Walter Ulbricht, would be left. With so many engineers gone the East Germans had to cancel their major prestige project, a new jet airliner. Khrushchev refused either to bribe the East Germans to stay or to tolerate the collapse of East Germany. Considering West Berlin a relic of the temporary 1945 settlement. Khrushchev thought that a peace treaty would end its status. As the Western powers had no intention of leaving, Khrushchev, from November 1958, threatened to sign a peace with the East

Germans and then expel the Westerners. The tiny garrison of West Berlin could not possibly rebuff the massive Soviet army. President Eisenhower considered all of this academic; nothing in Europe was worth risking the nuclear war that such an attack would probably cause. Periodically he sent his Secretary of State, John Foster Dulles, to declare that attacking West Berlin would cause nuclear war. Meetings about the status of the city were allowed to end inconclusively.

Taking office in January 1961, his successor, President Kennedy, was far less confident. He considered the lack of any real option short of nuclear war frightening rather than comforting.

In February Khrushchev announced that a peace treaty had to be signed before West German elections that autumn. When he met Kennedy in June, Khrushchev demanded a settlement by December. Kennedy announced that he would fight to hold West Berlin. Khrushchev noticed that Kennedy was not demanding continued access to the whole city. All that mattered was that West Berlin remain safe.

Khrushchev ordered the construction of a wall, about 100 miles long, to shut in East Berliners. Manned by 15,000 guards, it became the most potent symbol of the Cold War, splitting friend from friend, breaking up streets. East Germans

ABOVE Pin commemorating 13 August 1961.

RIGHT Berlin Wall border crossing sign.

YOU ARE LEAVING THE AMERICAN SECTOR
ВЫ ВЫЕЗЖАЕТЕ ИЗ АМЕРИКАНСКОГО СЕКТОРА
VOUS SORTEZ DU SECTEUR AMÉRICAIN
SIE VERLASSEN DEN AMERIKANISCHEN SEKTOR

ABOVE AND RIGHT The East Germans became famous for their ruthlessness. When 18-year-old Peter Fechter was shot trying to get over the Wall on 17 August 1962, the East Germans made no attempt to help him, and the Westerners – who could see him – could do nothing during nearly an hour of agony. East German soldiers finally took his body away after he died.

BELOW Even some East German border guards, like 19-year-old Conrad Schumann, fled while they could, before the Wall was complete. This was at Bernauer Strasse in Berlin-Wedding, on 15 August 1961.

WALTER ULBRICHT (1893–1973)

Ulbricht led East Germany from 1950 to 1971. A thorough Stalinist, he opposed the relaxation Stalin's heirs demanded, and felt vindicated when the (unfulfilled) promise of better conditions led to the 1953 uprising. He was the prime advocate of the Berlin Wall, and in 1968 he committed East German forces to help put down the Prague Spring – which he considered a direct threat to his own power. He was forced out because of his opposition to Willy Brandt's opening to East Germany.

tried to tunnel under the Wall or climb over it. In Len Deighton's novel *Funeral in Berlin*, later adapted for the cinema, funerals were used as cover for escapes (with the escapees inside coffins). Of about 10,000 East Germans who tried to cross the Wall, about half succeeded, and about 600 were shot while trying. With the Wall in place, the East German government was able to extort money from West Germany to allow elderly citizens out to join their families in the West, exchanging about 3.5 billion marks for 250,000 people.

OPPOSITE President John F. Kennedy looks at the Wall, in June 1963. He had accepted the construction of the Wall (and the preservation of West Berlin) because the alternative, to risk war over Berlin, seemed far worse.

ON BEHALF OF MAJOR GENERAL RAYMOND E. HADDOCK, THE U.S. COMMANDER, BERLIN, AND DEPUTY CHIEF OF THE U.S. MISSION, BERLIN; AND BRIGADIER GENERAL C.G. MARSH, COMMANDER, BERLIN BRIGADE, AND COMMUNITY COMMANDER; WE WELCOME YOU TO CHECKPOINT CHARLIE.

THIS PACKET IS PROVIDED TO ASSIST YOU WHILE YOU ARE VISITING EAST BERLIN. INSTRUCTIONS IN THIS PACKET ARE DERIVED FROM APPLICABLE MILITARY REGULATIONS AND STATE DEPARTMENT INSTRUCTIONS.

PLEASE REMEMBER THAT YOU ARE REPRESENTING THE UNITED STATES GOVERNMENT. HIGH STANDARDS OF CONDUCT WILL ENHANCE THE MAINTENANCE OF OUR RIGHT OF FREE ACCESS TO ALL SECTORS OF BERLIN.

GARRY L. PITTMAN
LTC, MP
PROVOST MARSHAL

RIGHT, BELOW AND OPPOSITE Sample pages from the official pack for US troops passing through Checkpoint Charlie, with practical advice on visiting Communist-controlled East Berlin.

If you encounter US or other Allied travelers in trouble, render what assistance you may and notify the MPs at Checkpoint Charlie. If given an emergency notification slip, proceed directly to Checkpoint Charlie and give the slip to the US MPs located there.

VEHICLE BREAKDOWN:

*** Telephone Checkpoint Charlie at (849) 819-5459/5439, or the American Embassy at 220-2741.

*** Attempt to repair the vehicle.

*** Dispatch the emergency notification form to Checkpoint Charlie by means of any available Allied traveler and remain with your vehicle until the arrival of US recovery personnel.

TRAFFIC ACCIDENT:

*** If minor, attempt to settle it on the scene and report directly to Checkpoint Charlie.

*** If serious, or unable to settle minor accident, dipatch the emergency notification and indicate whether an ambulance and/or wrecker is needed.

NOTE: If East German police become involved in the investigation of an accident, do not help or hinder their investigation. Do not display or surrender any documents to the GDR authorities. If East German police request documentation from you, show them the flash card demanding your right to proceed. If this is denied, use the flash card requesting the presence of a Soviet Officer.

- 3 -

NOTE: IF YOU REQUEST THE PRESENCE OF A SOVIET OFFICER, YOU ARE REQUIRED TO WAIT AT THAT LOCATION FOR ONE HOUR REGARDLESS IF EAST GERMAN AUTHORITIES ALLOW YOU TO PROCEED. FAILURE TO WAIT ONE HOUR WILL RESULT IN A MILITARY POLICE REPORT BEING INITIATED AGAINST YOU AND AN ADMINISTRATIVE BAR TO TRAVEL WILL BE LEVIED AGAINST YOU.

*** If you have not requested an ambulance, wrecker, or Soviet Officer, you may proceed when East German authorities so indicate.

*** Emergency medical services may be accepted from Soviet or East German authorities if necessary.

If you are stopped and /or detained by East German authorities and are not involved in a traffic accident:

*** Attempt to proceed.

*** If the detention continues, show the flash card demanding your right to proceed. If this is to no avail, wait ten minutes and display it again.

*** If still detained, show the flash card requesting that a Soviet officer come to your location.

NOTE: IF YOU REQUEST THE PRESENCE OF A SOVIET OFFICER, YOU ARE REQUIRED TO WAIT AT THAT LOCATION FOR ONE HOUR REGARDLESS IF EAST GERMAN AUTHORITIES ALLOW YOU TO PROCEED. FAILURE TO WAIT ONE HOUR WILL RESULT IN A MILITARY POLICE REPORT BEING INITIATED AGAINST YOU AND AN ADMINSTRATIVE BAR TO TRAVEL WILL BE LEVIED AGAINST YOU.

- 4 -

BERLIN

SOVIET SECTOR

ZENTRUM

Allied Checkpoint Charlie

- U-Bahn
- S-Bahn
- Gaststätte
- Theater
- Museums
- Ausstellungsräume
- Bibliothek
- Reisebüro

1. Natural Sciences Museum
2. Charity·Hospital Medical School
3. GDR Academy of Fine Arts
4. German Theatre/Intimate Theatre
5. Frederickstown Palace Variety Theatre
6. Berlin Ensemble Theatre
7. Thistle Cabaret/Metropol Music Theatre
8. Metropol Hotel
9. International Trade Center
10. Brandenburg Gate
11. Soviet Embassy
12. Comic Opera House
13. Postmaster-General Museum
14. "Under the Lime Trees" Inter-Hotel

15. German State Library
16. Humboldt University
17. Maxim Gorki Theatre
18. Main House of German-Soviet Friendship
19. Memorial for the Victims of Fascism and Militarism
20. Museum of German History
21. German State Opera House/Old Library
22. Academy Square
23. Central Committee of the Socialist Unity Party of Germany
24. Ministry of Foreign Affairs
25. Pergamon Museum
26. National Gallery

27. Old Museum
28. Palace of the Republic
29. Office of the GDR State Council
30. Palace Hotel
31. St. Mary's Church
32. German Post Office Radio & Television Tower
33. Berlin Civic Hall
34. GDR Council of Ministers
35. Ermeler House
36. Otto Nagel House
37. Brandenburgian Museum
38. Popular Theatre
39. "City of Berlin" Hotel & Alexander Platz shopping area

40. Keibelstrasse Parking Garage
41. GDR Travel Office/INTERFLUG Airline
42. Teacher's House/Congress Hall
43. "Berolina" Inter-Hotel/Theatre
44. Lenin Memorial
45. Memorial to Members of the German Inter-Brigades
46. Fairytale Fountain
47. Memorial to the Joint Combat of Polish Soldiers and German Anti-Fascists

→ Recommended Route to Downtown Area

BELOW AND RIGHT The cover and sample
pages from a Western propaganda booklet
distributed in East Berlin describing the day-by-
day build up to 13 August 1961. See Translations
on page 157.

Eine erste Stacheldrahtsperre an der Grenze zum französischen Sektor.

So setzt das kommunistische Regime seine „Volkspolizei" gegen „sein Volk" ein.

BELOW Classified Stasi document showing a cross-section of the Wall and listing its specifications, including length (162 km/101 miles), watchtowers and command posts (190) and anti-tank obstacles (38,000). See Translations on page 157.

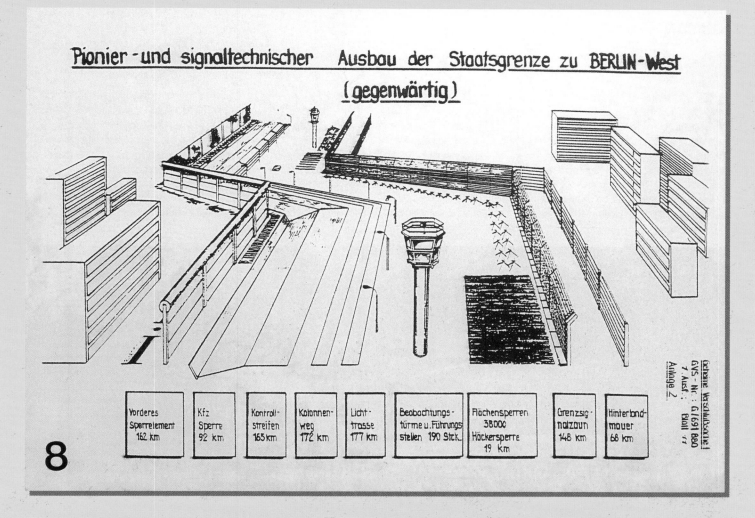

Pionier - und signaltechnischer   Ausbau der Staatsgrenze zu BERLIN-West
(gegenwärtig)

| Vorderes Sperrelement 162 km | Kfz Sperre 92 km | Kontroll-streifen 165 km | Kolonnen-weg 172 km | Licht-trasse 177 km | Beobachtungs-türme u. Führungs stellen 190 Stck. | Flächensperren 38000 Höckersperre 19 km | Grenzsig-nalzaun 148 km | Hinterland-mauer 68 km |

Geheime Verschlußsache!
GVS - Nr.: G 1691 880
7 Ausf., Blatt 11
Anlage 2

8

CHAPTER 17

CUBAN MISSILE CRISIS

Having survived Berlin, President Kennedy faced a worse crisis the following year.

Having survived Berlin, President Kennedy faced a worse crisis the following year. Khrushchev ordered medium- and intermediate-range nuclear missiles secretly placed in Cuba, a few minutes' flight time from the United States: 24 SS-4 launchers (36 missiles, range 1,100 nm) and 16 SS-5 launchers (24 missiles, range 2,400 nm), as well as defending fighters, surface-to-air missiles and

surface weapons. US intelligence failed – inexplicably – to detect the arrival of the missiles. Presented in October with photographs showing the ballistic missile bases nearing completion, Kennedy reacted furiously. His advisers suggested attacking the missile sites before they became operational. US nuclear strike forces were placed on alert. When a Soviet anti-aircraft missile site in Cuba shot down a US

U-2 photographing the island, there was talk of attacking its site. Nuclear war seemed imminent. Kennedy sought a less dangerous way to force the missiles out. He ordered a naval blockade of Cuba (which he called a quarantine, so that it was not formally an act of war). After a few very tense days and some careful diplomacy Khrushchev withdrew the missiles and promised never to base offensive weapons in Cuba.

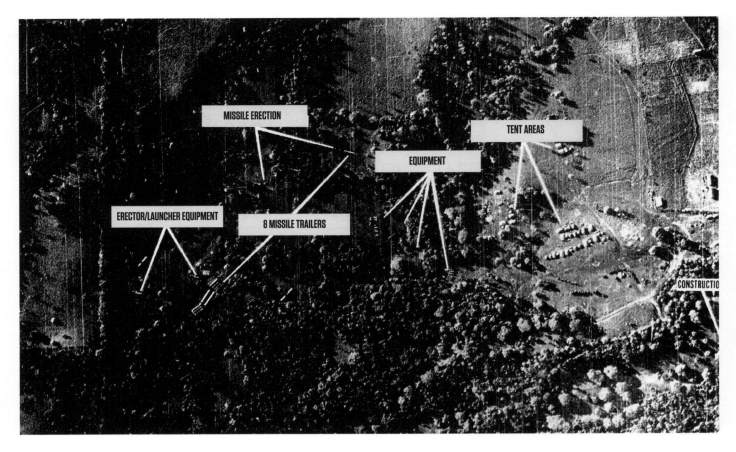

THE CUBAN MISSILE CRISIS OCTOBER 1962

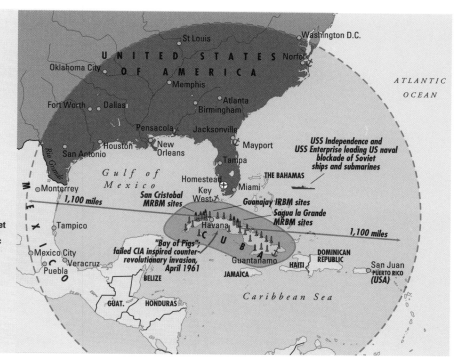

US blockade zone

Furthest extent of Soviet medium-range ballistic missiles (MRBM)

Soviet MRBM site

Soviet S-2 SAM site

US naval base

US Air Force base

USS Independence and USS Enterprise leading US naval blockade of Soviet ships and submarines

San Cristobal MRBM sites

Guanajay IRBM sites

Sagua la Grande MRBM sites

"Bay of Pigs", failed CIA inspired counter-revolutionary invasion, April 1961

1,100 miles

1,100 miles

LEFT Photographs like these helped convince Kennedy that the Soviets really had placed missiles in Cuba. The situation was so serious that they were released to the world to demonstrate what was happening; otherwise they would have been withheld to avoid giving away US capabilities.

ABOVE Decision: American policy was worked out by the Executive Committee (EXCOMM) of the National Security Council. The President's brother, Robert F. Kennedy was a key advisor.

ABOVE As the Soviets withdrew their missiles, US warships and aircraft checked that they were really carrying them. Here the US destroyer *Vesole* comes alongside the Soviet freighter *Polzunov* – a Liberty Ship given by the United States to the Soviet Union during World War II, when the two were allied.

Kennedy's administration believed (incorrectly, as it turned out) that the Soviets already had enough long-range ballistic missiles to destroy key cities in the United States. To the Soviets that made Kennedy's violent reaction proof that the Americans were unpredictable and dangerous; they had better be cautious lest they provoke war. Thus, during the Vietnam War, a few years later, the Soviets feared conflict intensifying to nuclear war (which was never remotely possible) until the United States agreed to peace talks in 1968. American intelligence never appreciated that the United States enjoyed this advantage.

Kennedy seems to have been reacting to American political realities – by October 1962 the mid-term Congressional campaign was well under way. As a Democrat, he felt vulnerable to Republican charges that he had ignored earlier information that missiles were being moved into

Cuba. He had done so in July partly on the basis of Soviet assurances. Now the President felt betrayed and vulnerable.

Nor did the Americans understand why the missiles had been put into Cuba; they supposed that they offered the Soviets some special advantage, perhaps due to the very short time it would take a missile to reach Washington from Cuba. In fact, Khrushchev had learned that his ICBM programme was a shambles. He was inspired by the earlier deployment of US intermediate-range missiles to Turkey – which made up for delays in the American ICBM system. Khrushchev agreed to withdraw his missiles from Cuba only after Kennedy secretly agreed to withdraw US missiles from Turkey. To save Kennedy's face, the withdrawal from Turkey was announced long enough after the Soviet withdrawal so that that they did not seem related.

Khrushchev never consulted Castro when he agreed to withdraw the missiles: to the Soviets, he was no more independent than any of the puppet rulers of Eastern Europe. Castro feared that he might be abandoned altogether for some Soviet "accommodation" with the Americans. One way to make himself indispensable was to stay at the forefront of the "world revolution" the Soviets claimed to support. That may explain why it was the Cubans, not the Russians, who in the 1970s fought for African revolutionaries in Angola and Mozambique – a point not understood in the United States (where the Cubans were seen simply as Soviet proxies).

After the crisis, US intelligence gradually realized just how badly the Soviet long-range missile programme was going, and how vulnerable the existing ones were. The secret that the United States had an excellent chance of destroying the entire Soviet strategic strike system if it attacked first was known to the most senior officials of the Johnson and Nixon administrations. When the US advantage disappeared about 1969, President Nixon sought the first of the Cold War nuclear arms limitation agreements.

ABOVE Strategic Air Command personnel interpreting reconnaissance in 1962 during the Cuban Missile Crisis.

THE SOVIET SS-6 ICBM

This development was authorized in 1954; it first flew in 1957. It surprised US experts by being developed instead of a shorter-range MRBM; the trick was to group rocket engines (which might have powered the smaller missile) together to obtain enough thrust. The result was really too clumsy for a weapon, but it was and remains a very reliable space booster. At the time of the Cuban Missile Crisis, the entire Soviet long-range missile arsenal was probably four or five of these weapons.

BELOW A map of Cuba, with a partial listing of Soviet
military equipment, used during President Kennedy's
meetings with political and military advisors on
17 October.

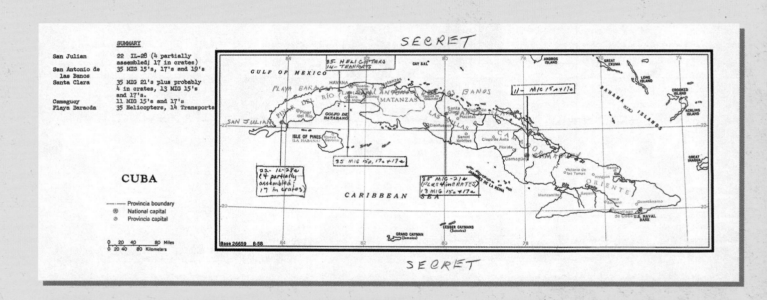

SUMMARY

San Julian	22 IL-28 (4 partially assembled; 17 in crates)
San Antonio de las Banos	35 MIG 15's, 17's and 19's
Santa Clara	35 MIG 21's plus probably 4 in crates, 13 MIG 15's and 17's.
Camaguey	11 MIG 15's and 17's
Playa Baracda	35 Helicopters, 14 Transports

CUBA

----- Provincia boundary
⊛ National capital
⊙ Provincia capital

0 20 40   80 Miles
0 20 40   80 Kilometers

THE WHITE HOUSE

WASHINGTON

October 22, 1962

Sir:

A copy of the statement I am making tonight concerning developments in Cuba and the reaction of my Government thereto has been handed to your Ambassador in Washington. In view of the gravity of the developments to which I refer, I want you to know immediately and accurately the position of my Government in this matter.

In our discussions and exchanges on Berlin and other international questions, the one thing that has most concerned me has been the possibility that your Government would not correctly understand the will and determination of the United States in any given situation, since I have not assumed that you or any other sane man would, in this nuclear age, deliberately plunge the world into war which it is crystal clear no country could win and which could only result in catastrophic consequences to the whole world, including the aggressor.

At our meeting in Vienna and subsequently, I expressed our readiness and desire to find, through peaceful negotiation, a solution to any and all problems that divide us. At the same time, I made clear that in view of the objectives of the ideology to which you adhere, the United States could not tolerate any action on your part which in a major way disturbed the existing over-all balance of power in the world. I stated that an attempt to force abandonment of our responsibilities and commitments in Berlin would constitute such an action and that the United States would resist with all the power at its command.

It was in order to avoid any incorrect assessment on the part of your Government with respect to Cuba that I publicly stated that if certain developments in Cuba took place, the United States would do whatever must be done to protect its own security and that of its allies.

- 2 -

Moreover, the Congress adopted a resolution expressing its support of this declared policy. Despite this, the rapid development of long-range missile bases and other offensive weapons systems in Cuba has proceeded. I must tell you that the United States is determined that this threat to the security of this hemisphere be removed. At the same time, I wish to point out that the action we are taking is the minimum necessary to remove the threat to the security of the nations of this hemisphere. The fact of this minimum response should not be taken as a basis, however, for any misjudgement on your part.

I hope that your Government will refrain from any action which would widen or deepen this already grave crisis and that we can agree to resume the path of peaceful negotiation.

Sincerely,

His Excellency
Nikita S. Khrushchev
Chairman of the Council of Ministers
  of the Union of Soviet Socialist Republics
MOSCOW

BELOW US State Department translation of Khrushchev's 23 October
reply to Kennedy.

SECRET

DEPARTMENT OF STATE
DIVISION OF LANGUAGE SERVICES

(TRANSLATION)

LS NO. 45989
T-85/T-94
Russian

[Embossed Seal of the USSR]

Moscow, October 23, 1962

Mr. President:

I have just received your letter, and have also acquainted myself
with the text of your speech of October 22 regarding Cuba.

I must say frankly that the measures indicated in your statement
constitute a serious threat to peace and to the security of nations. The
United States has openly taken the path of grossly violating the United
Nations Charter, the path of violating international norms of freedom of
navigation on the high seas, the path of aggressive actions both against
Cuba and against the Soviet Union.

The statement by the Government of the United States of America can
only be regarded as undisguised interference in the internal affairs of
the Republic of Cuba, the Soviet Union and other states. The United
Nations Charter and international norms give no right to any state to
institute in international waters the inspection of vessels bound for
the shores of the Republic of Cuba.

And naturally, neither can we recognize the right of the United
States to establish control over armaments which are necessary for the
Republic of Cuba to strengthen its defense capability.

We reaffirm that the armaments which are in Cuba, regardless of the
classification to which they may belong, are intended solely for defensive
purposes in order to secure the Republic of Cuba against the attack of an
aggressor.

His Excellency
    John Kennedy,
        President of the United States of America

SECRET

SECRET
-2-

I hope that the United States Government will display wisdom and
renounce the actions pursued by you, which may lead to catastrophic
consequences for world peace.

The viewpoint of the Soviet Government with regard to your statement
of October 22 is set forth in a Statement of the Soviet Government, which
is being transmitted to you through your Ambassador at Moscow.

[s] N. Khrushchev

N. Khrushchev

SECRET

OPPOSITE President Kennedy's public
statement on 28 October effectively ends the
13 days of the Cuban Missile Crisis.

IMMEDIATE RELEASE   October 28, 1962

Office of the White House Press Secretary
- -

THE WHITE HOUSE

STATEMENT BY THE PRESIDENT

I welcome Chairman Khrushchev's statesmanlike decision to stop building bases in Cuba, dismantling offensive weapons and returning them to the Soviet Union under United Nations verification. This is an important and constructive contribution to peace.

We shall be in touch with the Secretary General of the United Nations with respect to reciprocal measures to assure peace in the Caribbean area.

It is my earnest hope that the governments of the world can, with a solution of the Cuban crisis, turn their urgent attention to the compelling necessity for ending the arms race and reducing world tensions. This applies to the military confrontation between the Warsaw Pact and NATO countries as well as to other situations in other parts of the world where tensions lead to the wasteful diversion of resources to weapons of war.

# # # # # # # #

CHAPTER 18

VIETNAM

To Europeans, Vietnam did not seem part of the Cold War. Americans argued that while Vietnam itself might not be vital, if it fell countries whose natural resources really were vital to the West would collapse: Thailand, Malaysia, Burma, and Indonesia.

This "domino theory" was derided, but arguably the fight for South Vietnam bought time the other countries needed to become strong enough to survive.

The war grew out of the failed French attempt to regain their Indo-Chinese colony after the defeat of the Japanese in World War II. American reluctance to supply France (for what seemed at the time not to be part of the Cold War) embittered the French. After defeating the French at Dien Bien Phu, the Communists took over North Vietnam, but not South Vietnam or neighbouring Laos and Cambodia, which they still hoped to win.

By 1959 Communists in South Vietnam were losing their fight. They appealed to the North Vietnamese for help. As nominal head of the world Communist movement, Khrushchev vetoed such armed struggle for fear that it might touch off a nuclear holocaust. Given the split between Soviets and Chinese, the North Vietnamese did not feel bound by Khrushchev's order.

In 1963 President Kennedy's administration secretly sponsored a coup against South Vietnamese Premier Ngô Đình Diệm, who, it considered, was losing the war. That in effect made the US responsible for South Vietnam.

HO CHÍ MINH (1890–1969)

Ho Chí Minh created Vietnam, initially leading rebels against the French. During World War II he fought the Japanese, and he thought he had secured an agreement from his American supporters that he would form an independent Vietnam afterwards. Negotiations with the French collapsed, beginning a war he won in 1954. Once in power, he brutally suppressed a peasant rebellion, to create a Communist state. By 1964 his control was complete enough to maintain order under the stress of a gruesome and lengthy war, the victory of which he did not live to see.

OPPOSITE One enduring image of war in Vietnam is US firepower directed at areas rather than at enemy individuals. The hope was that massive bombardment of their sanctuaries would demoralize the enemy. Here B-52s bomb jungle areas in which the Viet Cong were thought to be operating.

BELOW Vietnam changed warfare by showing how helicopters could move troops around a largely roadless country – as long as they were armed well enough to survive (as shown here in Danang in March 1965). The Soviets provided the North Vietnamese with hand-held anti-aircraft missiles, the predecessors of those the Afghan guerrillas would later wield so effectively against Soviet helicopters.

1959
JANUARY: NORTH VIETNAMESE DECIDE TO SUPPORT ARMED STRUGGLE IN THE SOUTH

1961
OCTOBER: PRESIDENT KENNEDY DECIDES TO FIGHT IN SOUTH VIETNAM

1963
1 NOVEMBER: COUP IN SOUTH VIETNAM; NGÔ ĐÌNH DIỆM KILLED

1965
8 MARCH: FIRST US UNITS (3RD MARINES) TO SOUTH VIETNAM

1968
31 JANUARY: TET OFFENSIVE

1972
30 MARCH: NORTH VIETNAMESE BEGIN FAILED ATTACK ON SOUTH VIETNAM

1973
27 JANUARY: PEACE TREATY ENDS VIETNAM WAR

29 MARCH: LAST US TROOPS LEAVE SOUTH VIETNAM

1975
7 JANUARY: NORTH VIETNAMESE BEGIN SUCCESSFUL OFFENSIVE

30 APRIL: NORTH VIETNAMESE OCCUPY SAIGON

Soon afterwards the North Vietnamese decided to send army units into South Vietnam to back up the assistance already provided. Fearing US retaliation, the North Vietnamese sought modern air defences. The Soviets, the only potential source, turned them down and withdrew their ambassador. However, using the threat that the rest of the world movement would see them as cowards, the North Vietnamese forced them to reverse course. Soon the Soviets were supplying the bulk of what North Vietnam needed, without gaining much control over the war. By this time Communist forces largely controlled Laos, funnelling supplies into South Vietnam through it and through Cambodia.

By 1965 US ground formations were fighting North Vietnamese troops and Viet Cong guerrillas. Fear of Chinese intervention (as in Korea) precluded any invasion of North Vietnam, the source of the war. The US government seemed not to be fighting the war wholeheartedly. Even the massive bombing campaign against North

Vietnam was drastically limited. For example, anti-aircraft missile sites under construction could not be attacked for fear of killing the Chinese troops building them. For most of the war, attacks on the key harbour of Haiphong were barred for fear of sinking Soviet ships. Even so, at the peak of the war 500,000 US troops were in Vietnam; in all about 58,000 Americans died (47,000 in combat). The South Vietnamese forces lost 224,000; allies (South Korea, Thailand, Australia and New Zealand) lost another 5,300. The North Vietnamese/Viet Cong lost 1.1 million, but total deaths, including those in the North, may have been 4 million.

The war was frustrating for the Americans and the South Vietnamese; the enemy did not feel compelled to hold ground, but could melt away at will. Reports of corruption in South Vietnam and of incompetence in the South Vietnamese army, were deeply discouraging. A powerful anti-war movement in the United States arose; to some extent the North Vietnamese won their war in the United States.

In the 1968 Tet Offensive the Viet Cong finally risked what they hoped would be a decisive battle in the cities of South Vietnam, particularly the capital, Saigon, and the old imperial capital, Hué. They were badly beaten, but to many the extent of the offensive showed that the war was unwinnable. With the Viet Cong gone, however, much of the country was secured and the Americans began withdrawal. US and South

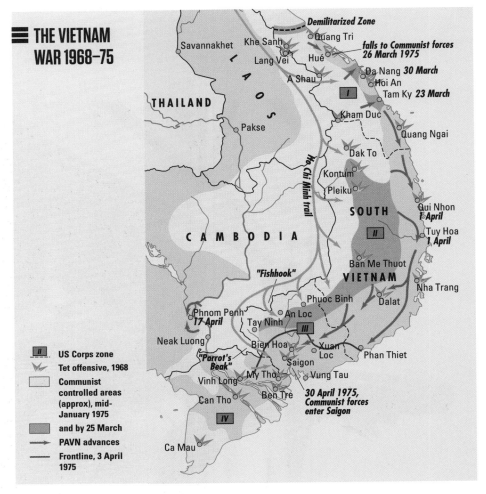

THE VIETNAM WAR 1968–75

falls to Communist forces 26 March 1975

Da Nang **30 March**
Tam Ky **23 March**

Qui Nhon **1 April**
Tuy Hoa **1 April**

Phnom Penh **17 April**

30 April 1975, Communist forces enter Saigon

II	US Corps zone
	Tet offensive, 1968
	Communist controlled areas (approx), mid-January 1975
	and by 25 March
→	**PAVN advances**
—	**Frontline, 3 April 1975**

Vietnamese forces defeated a 1972 North Vietnamese invasion across the Demilitarized Zone between the two countries. By then the US public saw little point in continuing the war. Congress imposed stronger and stronger restrictions on any further US involvement. When the North Vietnamese invaded again in 1975, this time through Laos and the Demilitarized Zone, Congress barred President Gerald Ford from helping. South Vietnam collapsed.

LEFT For Americans, the final humiliation was to watch the remaining US officials climb to the roof of their embassy to escape approaching North Vietnamese troops. It was too late to evacuate many of the South Vietnamese who had supported their pro-US government.

BELOW In February 1968 the Viet Cong attacked the main cities of South Vietnam; it took some very hard fighting to beat them back. Here wounded Marines ride a tank in Hué. The battles destroyed the Viet Cong, but the local US command, which wanted more troops, portrayed them as a disaster, with serious consequences in the United States.

LYNDON B. JOHNSON (1908–1973)

Johnson was a gifted politician caught in a war he did not want, unable to see any way out. His great wish was to effect social change in the United States, attacking racial discrimination and poverty. Thinking that war stemmed from a general desire for prosperity, in 1965 he tried to end the Vietnam War by offering a Mekong Delta development scheme. He turned against the war when, after it had put down the Tet Offensive, the US Army demanded 200,000 more men, suggesting that the war was unwinnable.

CHAPTER 19

THE PRAGUE SPRING

By the mid-1960s the Central European Communist countries were in serious economic trouble because their political orthodoxy overrode economic reality.

Decisions were geared to political demands and rewards, not efficiency. Worse, as an extension of the Soviet state, the Party concentrated on producing what the Soviet Union needed, and selling it to the Soviets, often well below the cost of production. Czechoslovakia had some of the worst problems because its Party boss, Antonín Novotný, was one of the most orthodox. In 1963 his country's national income

declined for the first time in the Soviet bloc. Initially the Party resisted calls for reform by reducing central planning (i.e., the Party's control of the Czechoslovak economy). However, the problem was so obvious that the Party felt forced to appoint a new leader, Alexander Dubček, who was expected to limit reforms and so preserve the Party's power. Dubček soon realized that he had to open up the system to create "socialism

with a human face". That face smiled on many of those who in other Communist countries would have been condemned. Emboldened Czechoslovak intellectuals and students demanded more radical changes. This was far more than the Party had bargained for. Worst of all, Czechoslovakia had an open border with Ukraine in the Soviet Union (and many Ukrainians could understand Czechoslovak radio broadcasts).

ABOVE Soviet armoured forces patch

RIGHT Alexander Dubček never believed the Soviets would invade, as long as he avoided the mistakes the Hungarians had made in 1956. This was his last meeting with Brezhnev (and his last warning).

Communist bosses in the East European satellite countries complained to Moscow that their positions were being undermined. They found a willing listener in Leonid Brezhnev, who had succeeded Khrushchev after a 1964 coup. Demands by the East Europeans seem to have convinced a slightly hesitant Brezhnev to act. He proclaimed the "Brezhnev Doctrine": the Soviet Union would not stand by if Communism were threatened anywhere that it had taken root. He decided to invade Czechoslovakia to restore orthodox Communism.

Of the governments Brezhnev consulted, only Romania refused to participate (Brezhnev considered invading her, too). In effect, the Romanians withdrew from the Warsaw Pact, telling the Americans that they intended not to become involved in any Warsaw Pact attack, that they were not allowing Soviet nuclear weapons on their soil — and therefore that they hoped very much to be left out of any NATO nuclear targeting. The Romanians did retain formal membership in the Pact and they continued to receive new weapons (some of

which they sold to Western intelligence).

Attacking in August 1968, the combined Communist army of almost half a million met little overt resistance, although Czechoslovak radio stations and newspapers survived for about a week. Probably 83 were killed throughout the country, and several thousand were arrested. Having agreed not to resist, Dubček was allowed to stay in power. He was removed a year later after Czechoslovaks staged mass demonstrations nominally celebrating their defeat of a Soviet hockey team. Later he was expelled from the Czechoslovak Communist Party, but he was not imprisoned.

Western military experts were shocked by the invasion of Czechoslovakia. Preparations had been very successfully masked by a large training exercise. They had assumed that NATO would enjoy considerable warning of any Soviet-led attack. It would give NATO enough time to call up reserves, which were its real strength. Without those reserves, NATO could not counter a non-nuclear Soviet invasion. Was it now possible for the Soviets to attack suddenly, by

ABOVE Soviet tanks occupied Prague, and some of the Czechs fought back. Most, however, did not; perhaps they remembered how badly Budapest had been damaged.

ALEXANDER DUBČEK (1921–1992)

He fought in the wartime underground and then rose through the Czech Communist Party to become First Secretary in 1968. Brought in to replace a Stalinist predecessor, he surprised his patrons by deciding that the problem was the Party itself, with its careerism and its rigidity. He was probably the most surprised of all that "socialism with a human face" was perceived as a great threat to every other country's orthodox Communism. Later he said that Brezhnev had deceived him by denying any intent to invade.

RIGHT Soviet tanks line up in Prague after the invasion. This show of force seems to have convinced most Czechs that active resistance was pointless.

surprise? To win without risking nuclear annihilation?

The Soviet Union suffered from many of the same problems as Czechoslovakia. What would happen if it chose a Dubček as its leader, and if there were no consortium of Communist armies to unseat him? In about 20 years the world found out.

In the West, the Soviet-led invasion attracted widespread attention and condemnation, particularly heightened, later, by the shocking self-immolation of the philosophy student Jan Palach in protest against his country's loss of freedom. The summer of 1968 also coincided with widespread student unrest in Western countries, including what looked like a revolution in Paris which began as a protest over students' living and working conditions.

PARIS RIOTS

In May 1968 Paris exploded in student riots. Due to the post-war baby boom and prosperity, an unprecedented number of students had to share grossly inadequate facilities. The students were also enraged that the French economy could not produce enough jobs for them. An attempt to put down the students brought on a general strike by Communist-led unions. The Communists then found that they had little power over union members, who rejected the deal that they extracted from the French government. Ultimately, the riots and the strike demonstrated just how fragile France was. The same divisions which had almost destroyed the state in 1946 (when a Communist rising seemed imminent) were still present. President de Gaulle survived the riots, but resigned less than a year later when reforms he advocated were not passed.

RIGHT Famous edition of *Rudé Právo*, the official Czechoslovak Communist Party newspaper sympathetic at that time, in 1968, to Dubček's reforms, published on the day after Soviet and other Eastern Bloc tanks rolled into Czechoslovakia. The Stop Press section, top right, is an announcement by the Presidium of the Central Committee of the Czechoslovak Communist Party advising people to stay calm and not to resist the troops, but making clear that it considers the invasion to be contrary to the "basic norms of international law". The newspaper staff did not have time to print anything beyond page 1. See Translations on page 157.

OPPOSITE Anti-Soviet poster from 1968 which reads, "I cannot see, hear or speak, under occupation!"

ZVLÁŠTNÍ VYDÁNÍ

Proletáři všech zemí, spojte se!

RUDÉ PRÁVO

ORGÁN ÚSTŘEDNÍHO VÝBORU KOMUNISTICKÉ STRANY ČESKOSLOVENSKA

VE STŘEDU 21. SRPNA 1968 | ČÍSLO 231 — ROČNÍK 48 (Právo lidu roč. 71)

Všemu lidu Československé socialistické republiky!

Včera dne 20. 8. 1968 kolem 23. hod. večer překročila vojska Sovětského svazu, Polské lidové republiky, Německé demokratické republiky, Maďarské lidové republiky a Bulharské lidové republiky státní hranice Československé socialistické republiky. Stalo se tak bez vědomí presidenta republiky, předsedy Národního shromáždění, předsedy vlády i prvního tajemníka ÚV KSČ a těchto orgánů.

V těchto hodinách zasedalo předsednictvo ÚV KSČ a zabývalo se přípravou XIV. sjezdu strany. Předsednictvo ÚV KSČ vyzývá všechny občany naší republiky, aby zachovali klid a nekladli postupujícím vojskům odpor. Proto ani naše armáda, Bezpečnost a Lidové milice nedostaly rozkaz k obraně země.

Předsednictvo ÚV KSČ považuje tento akt za odporující nejenom všem zásadám vztahů mezi socialistickými státy, ale za popření základních norem mezinárodního práva.

Všichni vedoucí funkcionáři státu, KSČ i Národní fronty zůstávají ve svých funkcích, do nichž byli jako představitelé lidu a členů svých organizací zvoleni podle zákonů a jiných norem, platných v Československé socialistické republice.

Ústavními činiteli je okamžitě svoláváno zasedání Národního shromáždění, vlády republiky, předsednictvo ústředního výboru KSČ svolává plénum ÚV KSČ k projednání vzniklé situace.

PŘEDSEDNICTVO ÚV KSČ

Svaz měst a obcí

Fond republiky vzrůstá

NA VALNÉ HROMADĚ V BRNĚ USTAVEN
Hospodářský svaz státních statků

VE VÝCHODNÍCH ČECHÁCH
rehabilitace na postupu

VYSOKÁ OBJEKTIVNOST V KAŽDÉM PŘÍPADĚ ● CENNÉ ZKUŠENOSTI ČLENŮ KONTROLNÍ A REVIZNÍ KOMISE ● ODPOVĚDNÝ PŘÍSTUP NA ZÁVODECH

TELEGRAMY ZE SVĚTA

HISTORICI SVĚTA K MNICHOVSKÉ SMLOUVĚ
Vědecky o mezinárodní politice

Prostor pro rozvoj a svobodu
Místopředseda vlády dr. G. Husák mezi žiarskými hutníky

Významné archeologické nálezy u Loun

Zemědělský charakter všech osídlení ● Již před 6000 lety se v Poohří lidé živili obděláváním půdy

Stravování na chmelu

Geologický kongres pracovně

Oficiální expozice na brněnském veletrhu

Redakční kolektiv Rudého práva

Mudroch a V. Hložník národními umělci

Foto M. BUDIL

NEVIDÍM
NESLYŠÍM
NEMLUVÍM
S OKUPANTY !

CHAPTER 20

DETENTE: PEAK OF SOVIET POWER

While the United States dissipated its military resources in Vietnam, the Soviets invested in new long-range missiles in hardened silos, reversing the strategic advantage Kennedy had enjoyed during the Cuban crisis.

In 1965 the United States had 934 ICBMs, mostly lightweight Minutemen, as well as 464 submarine-launched missiles. It estimated that the Soviets had 224 ICBMs and 107 very inferior submarine-launched weapons; even that situation was far better than what Khrushchev had faced in 1962. Late in President Richard Nixon's first year in office, 1969, the Soviets had 1,109 ICBMs; the US programme had ended at 1,054. Many of the Soviet missiles were huge SS-9s. All were in hardened silos, whereas the 1965 missiles had been vulnerable to a US first strike. The Soviets had 240 submarine-launched ballistic missiles, compared to 656 for the United States.

President Nixon felt compelled to maintain amicable relations with the Soviets even as they supplied weapons which were killing Americans in Vietnam. Uncomfortably aware of how dangerous the prospect of nuclear war had become, Nixon and his Soviet counterpart, Leonid Brezhnev, were both very careful not to let a Middle East war in 1973 (Israel against Egypt and Syria) intensify. Nixon's chief foreign policy adviser, Dr Henry Kissinger, called the new arrangement détente, meaning an easing of strained relations between the superpowers. That included signing the 1972 Strategic Arms Limitation Treaty (SALT), which seemed to ratify Soviet strategic superiority. Negotiations had begun soon after Nixon became President in 1969.

Many Europeans concluded that the Soviets no longer presented any threat, ignoring the

ABOVE Nixon's only counter to the Soviets was to befriend the Chinese; he was uniquely well placed to do so because no one could doubt his anti-Communist credentials. Here he meets Mao Zedong on 22 February 1972.

less pleasant features of the Soviet system. It became popular to imagine that over time the two social systems might come to resemble each other. Willy Brandt's West German government, pursuing a policy of Ostpolitik, formally recognized East Germany. That was a step towards the Soviet goal of having the West ratify their occupation of Eastern Europe. The necessary treaty, work on which had begun

HENRY A. KISSINGER (1923–).

Dr Kissinger first became prominent as a nuclear strategist. He was President Nixon's National Security Advisor and then Secretary of State, identified with the policy of détente (which conservatives considered far too accommodating) but also with the policy of escalation (to force a settlement) in Vietnam and also with the US attacks on Chile's Salvador Allende (which opponents argue was the cause of his fall). Liberals considered Kissinger far too cynical, and conservatives considered him far too willing to accept Soviet power.

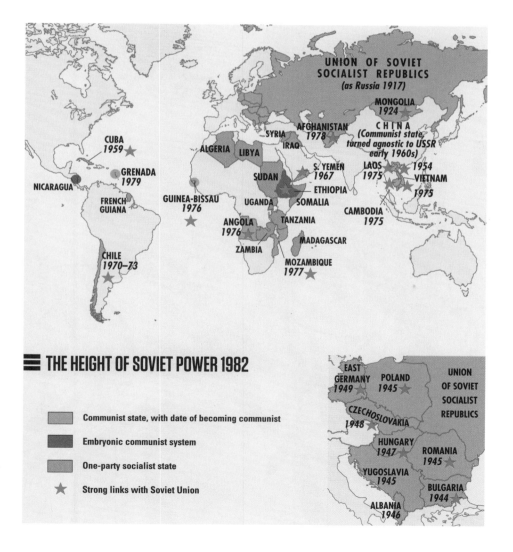

THE HEIGHT OF SOVIET POWER 1982

- Communist state, with date of becoming communist
- Embryonic communist system
- One-party socialist state
- ★ Strong links with Soviet Union

1970
12 AUGUST: WEST GERMAN NON-AGGRESSION PACT WITH SOVIETS RECOGNIZES DIVISION OF EUROPE

1972
21 FEBRUARY: NIXON VISITS CHINA, BREAKING ENMITY BETWEEN THE TWO COUNTRIES

26 MAY: US AND SOVIET UNION SIGN SALT I ARMS LIMITATION TREATY RECOGNIZING SOVIET NUMERICAL SUPERIORITY

22 NOVEMBER: HELSINKI CONFERENCE BEGINS

1973
11 MAY: WEST GERMANY RECOGNIZES EAST GERMANY

6 OCTOBER: MIDDLE EAST WAR BEGINS: SUPERPOWERS CO-OPERATE TO FORCE AN END

1974
25 APRIL: COUP IN PORTUGAL OPENS UP LAST EUROPEAN COLONIES IN AFRICA

1975
1 AUGUST: HELSINKI FINAL ACT RECOGNIZES DIVISION OF EUROPE

NOVEMBER: ATTEMPTED PRO-SOVIET COUP IN PORTUGAL

NOVEMBER: CUBAN-BACKED MPLA PROCLAIMED THE GOVERNMENT OF ANGOLA

in 1972, was duly signed by 35 countries at Helsinki in 1975. The only Soviet concession, which they apparently regarded as laughable, was to accept a "basket" of human rights. However, in Eastern Europe the "Helsinki basket" inspired many to brave repression in the name of human rights, and this movement was ultimately very important in places such as Poland.

The Soviets found that the West did not resist pro-Soviet coups and revolutions outside Europe – in countries which offered real advantages if they ever fought the West. Libya and Algeria provided bases on the Mediterranean. Angola and Mozambique lay athwart the tanker route around South Africa. Yemen could block the route through the Suez Canal. Angola and Mozambique offered sanctuary to guerrillas fighting in South Africa, the richest prize in Africa. Were they, too, Soviet proxies? We now know that in much of Africa the Soviets were concerned mainly to counter Chinese attempts to gain influence. Without an occupying army, Soviet control was limited. To Westerners, however, it seemed clear that the Soviet Union was the rising superpower.

Soviet success abroad masked serious domestic problems. To keep restive populations happy, they borrowed money to buy consumer goods from the West. Ostensibly the money would modernize industry, whose profits would

WILLY BRANDT (1913–92)

Brandt created the policy of Ostpolitik: accommodation with the Soviets and East Germans in return for guaranteed security for West Germany and West Berlin. To do that he had to recognize the massive losses of territory to Poland and to the Soviet Union after World War II, which previous German governments had resisted. He was mayor of West Berlin, then German Foreign Minister, becoming Chancellor in 1969. Brandt was brought down in 1974 when his closest adviser, Günter Guillaume, was revealed as an East German spy.

ABOVE The Soviets enforced détente by building massive strategic forces Americans felt they could not match. This "Typhoon" missile submarine was by far the largest in the world. In 1974, Brezhnev told American President Gerald Ford that unless he abandoned plans for his own new submarine missile system, Trident, he would face something far worse in the form of Typhoon.

OPPOSITE The combination of new Soviet strength and American wariness in the wake of Vietnam made it possible for the Soviets to support pro-Communist rebels in Africa. This Cuban officer is in Angola, in February 1976.

pay back the loans. The problem was intractable because it was really political. The Party's managers often wasted their new machinery, while unpaid loans piled up. In 1981, for example, Poland needed to borrow $10–11 billion, of which $7–8 billion would pay interest on the existing outstanding loan. The Soviets gave Poland $4.5 billion in scarce hard (Western) currency that year merely to prevent the United States from using the loan request as a way of pressuring the Poles.

The Soviet Union suffered further because military production was swallowing so many resources. Yet its military leaders perceived a new kind of military weakness. By the late 1970s they perceived that the key to future war was the computer – which Western civilian industry was churning out, but which Soviet industry could not produce in quantity. Westerners, for whom computers were commonplace, could not imagine the extent to which the Soviet military sensed crisis.

MEMORANDUM

THE WHITE HOUSE

WASHINGTON

3/26 Returned

THE PRESIDENT HAS SEEN.

INFORMATION

TOP SECRET

May 23, 1969

MEMORANDUM FOR THE PRESIDENT

FROM: Henry A. Kissinger   *HK*

SUBJECT: Analysis of Strategic Arms Limitation Proposals

A member of my staff in analyzing preliminary results from
the current study of strategic arms limitation proposals has
tentatively concluded that:

    -- some of the options that have gained the greatest
popularity within the government would appear to give the
Soviet Union significant improvements in its retaliatory
capability;

    -- the most comprehensive proposal, one that bans both
MIRVs and ABMs, would leave U.S. retaliatory capability
unchanged but would improve Soviet retaliatory capability by
over 70 percent. It would leave them in a position where they
could kill more than half of the American people in a second
strike;

    -- the option that looks good to us in terms of retaliatory
measures, one that retains at least 500 ABM launchers, MIRVs,
and a large U.S. bomber force, may well not be acceptable to
the Soviet Union.

Proponents of the comprehensive proposals will argue that
we should not be concerned that an agreement increases Soviet
retaliatory capability. We will be deterred from attacking them
without an agreement, they point out, and improvements in the
Soviet deterrent cannot increase the threat to us. In fact, they
argue, allowing the Soviet deterrent to improve is a reasonable
price to pay to get an agreement, since our own retaliatory
capability would not be impaired. Also, other aspects of our

TOP SECRET

COMMENTS ON
STRATEGIC EXCHANGE ANALYSIS
NSSM 28

At least three relatively specific objectives have motivated interest in a strategic arms limitation agreement with the Soviet Union:

1. An agreement could freeze or codify strategic relationships in a manner which preserves "equality" at worst and a U.S. edge at best.

2. Since both nations may be on the verge of new strategic deployments, an agreement might mean significant budgetary savings compared to the situation that would prevail with no agreement.

3. An agreement could reduce uncertainties in the strategic relationship, making both sides less nervous about potential threats to its strategic capabilities.

The analysis done to date raises questions about whether these objectives can be met with the strategic arms limitation options that have been considered.

1. The following table compares strategic exchange results for 1978 if there is no agreement and if any of several possible agreements is reached.

This table shows that only if the Soviet Union is planning a large ABM deployment in the absence of an agreement will an agreement mean significant cost reductions for the Soviets. U.S. strategic budgets for the next decade, according to the analysis, are relatively insensitive to whether or not there is an agreement and to what kind of an agreement it is.

3. The analysis to date has not attempted to compare uncertainties and the costs of hedging against them with and without an agreement. Also, the study has not analyzed how unilateral U.S. policies might be used to stabilize the strategic relationship and reduce risks.

Thus, the analysis leaves unanswered the following questions:

-- In what ways can a strategic arms agreement be in the interests of the United States and its Allies?

-- Are there proposals other than the options considered which would better serve U.S. and Allied interests?

-- If we insist on maintaining the area protection provided by Safeguard, how many launchers must we retain, and how will this affect the strategic exchange results and the relative rankings of the options?

TOP SECRET

	NO ABMS				ABM Limited to 500 Spartan-type ABM Missiles			
No Agreement; U.S. Programmed Force vs. High Intelligence Projection of Soviet Forces	OPTION I (Basically a simple ICBM Freeze)	III (Comprehensive offensive and defensive limits but MIRVs allowed)	III-A (Allow Both Sides to Superharden Missile Silos)	IV (Comprehensive Offensive and defensive limits with no MIRVs)	OPTION I (Basically a simple ICBM Freeze)	III (Comprehensive offensive and defensive limits but MIRVs allowed)	III-A (Allow Both Sides to Superharden Missile Silos)	IV (Comprehensive offensive and defensive limits with no MIRVs)
U.S. Second Strike Capability (% Soviet people killed promptly) 40%	41%	40%	42%	38%	39%	39%	44%	29%
Soviet Second Strike Capability (% U.S. people killed promptly) 33%	51%	43%	57%	54%	41%	25%	54%	40%
Crisis Stability [a] U.S. Lives Saved by Striking First Instead of Second 32 mil	3 mil	18 mil		5 mil	11 mil	31 mil		19 mil
Soviet Lives Saved by Striking First Instead of Second -9 mil [b]	3 mil	0		-6 mil [b]	-2 mil [b]	-5 mil [b]		-8 mil [b]
U.S. Deaths in Nuclear War								
U.S. Strikes First: U.S. Deaths 87 mil	127 mil	111 mil		130 mil	117 mil	95 mil		107 mil
Soviets Strike First: U.S. Deaths 139 mil	142 mil [c]	142 mil [c]		141 mil	140 mil	140 mil		135 mil
Difference between U.S. and Soviets killed in Soviet First Strike (If -, Soviets lose more) 4 mil	12 mil	12 mil		17 mil	9 mil	8 mil		11 mil

[a] The strategic relationship is considered to be unstable if one side could save a significant number of its own people (more than 20-30 million) by striking first in a crisis instead of striking second.

[b] This means that the Soviets would lose more lives by striking first than by striking second. This is highly desirable from our point of view.

[c] The calcuations were done using a method which does not take into account fatalities above the 142 million level.

CHAPTER 21

AFGHANISTAN

In 1978 a pro-Soviet coup overthrew the neutralist government of Afghanistan, on the southern Soviet border. The new government called on Moscow for help against rebelling Muslim tribesmen.

The Soviets feared that, if the government fell, an anti-Soviet successor might infect the Muslims of the southern Soviet Union with dangerous ideas. Given their Cold War mindset, it seemed (falsely) to the Soviets that the Afghan rebellion was being sponsored by the West. Just as the Americans had experienced in Vietnam, so the Soviets soon concluded that the government they were backing was ineffective. Surely a competent Afghan government backed by real (i.e., Soviet) troops would quickly deal with a few "medieval" tribesmen. In December

BELOW Afghans opposing the Soviets were lightly armed, and moved by horse or motorcycle.

THE SOVIET INVASION OF AFGHANISTAN 1979–89

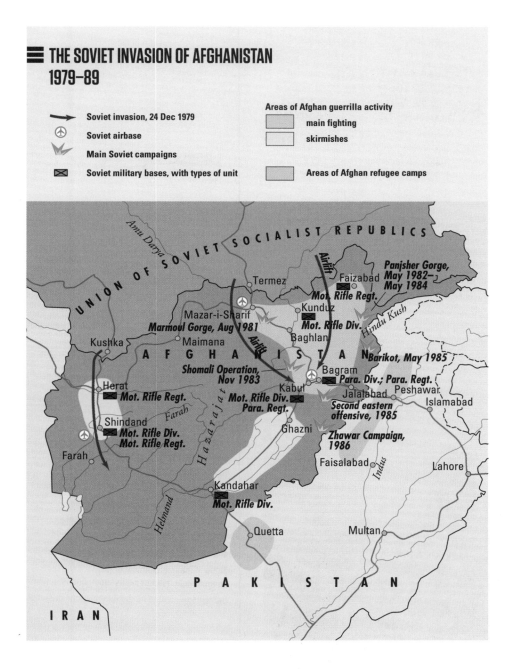

Soviet invasion, 24 Dec 1979

Soviet airbase

Main Soviet campaigns

Soviet military bases, with types of unit

Areas of Afghan guerrilla activity

main fighting

skirmishes

Areas of Afghan refugee camps

Amu Darya

UNION OF SOVIET SOCIALIST REPUBLICS

Termez

Faizabad

Panjsher Gorge, May 1982– May 1984

Airlift

Mot. Rifle Regt.

Kunduz

Mazar-i-Sharif

Marmoul Gorge, Aug 1981

Kushka

Maimana

Mot. Rifle Div.

Baghlan

Hindu Kush

AFGHANISTAN

Airlift

Shomali Operation, Nov 1983

Bagram

Barikot, May 1985

Para. Div.; Para. Regt.

Herat

Mot. Rifle Regt.

Kabul

Jalalabad

Peshawar

Islamabad

Second eastern offensive, 1985

Mot. Rifle Div. Para. Regt.

Hazarajat

Shindand

Farah

Mot. Rifle Div. Mot. Rifle Regt.

Ghazni

Zhawar Campaign, 1986

Indus

Farah

Faisalabad

Lahore

Helmand

Kandahar

Mot. Rifle Div.

Quetta

Multan

PAKISTAN

IRAN

1979 the Soviets invaded Afghanistan with 25,000 troops and overthrew its government, installing a new one that they had chosen. Soon the Soviets had about 100,000 troops in the country. By the time the Soviets left in 1989, almost 14,000 (22,000 according to some sources) had died.

The invasion seemed to confirm the view in the West that the Soviet Union had never given up its aggressive attitude. Surely the Soviets had chosen to invade Afghanistan in order to realize the old Russian dream of access to the warm waters of the Arabian Sea and the Persian Gulf. It also seemed that the Afghan operation was connected to the roughly simultaneous Iranian revolution: Iran was an old Russian objective. That the Soviets had already been deeply involved in Afghanistan since the 1978 coup, and that they were in effect maintaining the same policy, went unremarked. In any case, the Soviets were now annexing Afghanistan, and they might well decide to push further.

1978
27 APRIL: COUP INSTALLS PRO-SOVIET GOVERNMENT

1979
MARCH: AFGHAN GOVERNMENT ASKS FOR HELP TO DEAL WITH REBELS

12 DECEMBER: POLITBURO AUTHORIZES INTERVENTION IN "COUNTRY A"

24 DECEMBER: SOVIETS INVADE AND OVERTHROW EXISTING AFGHAN GOVERNMENT

1980
4 JANUARY: PRESIDENT CARTER ANNOUNCES EMBARGO ON SALES OF TECHNOLOGY TO SOVIET UNION

1981
20 JANUARY: RONALD REAGAN INAUGURATED AS PRESIDENT

1985
MARCH: REAGAN ORDERS INCREASED LETHAL AID TO AFGHAN REBELS

1988
8 FEBRUARY: SOVIETS ANNOUNCE WITHDRAWAL (BUT CONTINUED SUPPORT FOR THE AFGHAN GOVERNMENT)

1989
15 FEBRUARY: LAST SOVIET TROOPS LEAVE AFGHANISTAN

1992
15 APRIL: SOVIET-BACKED AFGHAN GOVERNMENT COLLAPSES

American President Jimmy Carter, an advocate of further arms control and détente, changed course. Among other things he ordered the defence budget increased. The proposed SALT II arms control treaty was scrapped. The Americans boycotted the 1980 Moscow Olympics (the hosting of which was a matter of great pride to the Soviets) in protest against the invasion. Carter also approved American aid to the Afghan guerrillas resisting the Soviets, despite some fears that helping them would cause the Soviets to retaliate elsewhere.

Even before Western aid made itself felt, many in the Soviet government felt that the war was unwinnable. The guerrillas were effective and they refused to give up: the Soviets could not kill enough of them to extinguish their movement and they could not occupy the whole country – nor could they attack Pakistan, the guerrillas'

main sanctuary and the immediate source of their arms. Failure was far worse than Vietnam had been for the Americans, because the Soviet empire (both inside and outside the Soviet Union) was held together by the threat of military force. If primitive tribesmen could defeat Soviet military power, surely others could, too. For the Politburo, the decisive argument against intervening in Poland was that it would be "Afghanistan in Europe" because, like the Afghans, the nationalistic Poles would surely fight. The Soviet situation in Afghanistan worsened drastically as, in the 1980s, the Americans (under Ronald Reagan) and the British (under Margaret Thatcher) greatly increased the level of aid to the guerrillas. In 1989 the Soviets felt compelled to withdraw their last troops, although they did continue to support the government they had installed in Kabul.

YURI V. ANDROPOV (1914–1984)

He was Stalin's expeditor in Korea, and in 1954 became ambassador to Hungary, responsible for suppressing the 1956 rebellion. He was then put in charge of relations with other governing Communist parties, and in 1967 became chairman of the KGB. He led the fight to intervene in Afghanistan. Leaving the KGB, he became Central Committee Secretary for Ideology, then succeeded Brezhnev as party leader. Once in office his main goal was to overcome the stagnation of the Brezhnev years, attacking alcoholism and absenteeism. Mikhail Gorbachev was his protégé.

LEFT Afghan anti-Soviet resistance fighters had primitive arms. The Afghans repulsed the then Red Army invasion with a huge human cost and with the material aid of the western world, above all, the United States. It is estimated that around one and a half million Afghans were killed in their fight against the Soviet soldiers.

It was one of many hand-launched infra-red guided anti-aircraft missiles which, from the Vietnam War onwards, made low altitudes very dangerous for aircraft. Such self-guided missiles provide a pilot with little or no warning. Aircraft therefore have to use counter-measures continuously, and they are armoured against the relatively small warhead a man-portable weapon can carry. Stingers supplied to the Afghan guerrillas effectively neutralized much of Soviet airpower. The current solution is for aircraft to rely on stand-off weapons.

CHAPTER 22
DISSIDENTS

The Soviet state always feared that intellectuals like those who had created it would turn dissident and destroy it.

The Soviet secret police, the KGB, deployed massive resources to detect those who refused to follow the Party's line. As in other police states, the KGB (and its equivalents in Eastern Europe) employed huge numbers of informers and wiretaps. To ensure loyalty, it secretly penetrated all official organizations (such as the military). It also tried to penetrate and thus to take over all dissident organizations, occasionally arresting their members. Such

BELOW Sirjanka detention camp in Yakutia, Siberia, in 1950. The conditions may seem spartan and clean, but the prisoners were systematically starved while being worked to death.

ALEKSANDR SOLZHENITSYN (1918–2008)

Solzhenitsyn was imprisoned in 1945 for casual remarks about Stalin, then allowed by Khrushchev to publish his unprecedented first novel about life in a prison camp. His Gulag Archipelago trilogy described the vast Soviet prison camp system and the maniacally random way in which they were populated under Stalin. Solzhenitsyn's experiences convinced him that any sort of progressive ideology leads in the end to that sort of inhumanity; ultimately he attacked both the West and the Soviet Union for this sin. He was expelled from the Soviet Union in 1974.

tactics were intended to convince anyone trying to form such a group that it was probably penetrated and therefore pointless. Contact with foreigners was particularly suspect. As an example of the scale of KGB operations, all visitors to the Soviet Union were followed and their telephones tapped as a matter of course. Stalin's regime relied largely on fear generated by random arrests and mass imprisonments, but such tactics were self-defeating. Stalin's successors almost immediately liberated most of the hundreds of thousands of political prisoners in Soviet concentration camps (gulags). Khrushchev went so far as to approve the publication of Aleksandr Solzhenitsyn's first novels describing Stalin's prison camps, *One Day in the Life of Ivan Denisovich* and *Cancer Ward*.

For Khrushchev's successors, this was going much too far. Denunciation of Stalin risked questioning the basis of the Soviet state. Instead of recreating Stalin's terror, they developed a focused approach.

The KGB sought out and arrested individual dissidents. Those who refused to recant were often sent to mental hospitals, where they were in effect tortured (the Soviets were eventually expelled from the World Psychiatric Congress for this practice). The official justification for such treatment was that anyone opposing the Soviet state literally had to be insane, since there could

be no escape from it. These tactics involved much smaller, though still quite significant, numbers than in Stalin's time. By 1985 there were 5,000–10,000 political prisoners in the Soviet Union, less than one per cent of Stalin's average.

The situation was further complicated by a new group of dissidents. After the 1967 Six Day War in the Middle East the Soviets broke off relations with Israel and began an anti-Semitic campaign within the Soviet Union. Soviet Jews tried to emigrate, but were blocked. They attracted foreign attention. In 1974 US Senator Henry Jackson managed to make trade relations (the Soviets needed American wheat) conditional on permitting Jews to emigrate, knowing that allowing any emigration at all would weaken the absolute control the Soviets felt they needed. This action infuriated those, like Dr Kissinger, seeking an accommodation with the Soviets. It showed other Soviet dissidents that their situation was not hopeless, because foreign pressure could be brought to bear on their government. For the Soviet authorities, this was more proof that it was vital to prevent contact between dissidents in the Soviet Union and Western media. Their existence and their words would be reported back into the Soviet Union by Western radio stations, which had a wide range of listeners despite official attempts to jam them.

Thus the most prominent dissident to remain in the Soviet Union, Andrei Sakharov (who had invented the Soviet hydrogen bomb), was forced into internal exile in the closed city of Gorkiy.

The attempt to eliminate (or at least to contain) all dissidence failed. The dissidents never really threatened the Soviet regime, not least because all of their groups were so thoroughly penetrated; but the dissident movement built up habits of thought which would become very significant once controls had weakened, under Mikhail Gorbachev. Moreover, the dissidents created a widely read underground literature, *samizdat* (self-published). It included Andrei Amalrik's prophetic *Will the Soviet Union Survive to 1984?*. The Soviet dissident movement had equivalents throughout Soviet-dominated Eastern Europe, the difference being that in other countries it had the added support of nationalists who could not accept Soviet domination. Dissident movements such as the Czechoslovak Charter 77 (inspired by the Helsinki Accord) and the Polish Solidarity became their countries' governments when Soviet domination collapsed.

ANDREI D. SAKHAROV (1921–1989)

Sakharov invented the Soviet hydrogen bomb, then tried to convince his country's rulers that they should renounce nuclear tests; he considered such weapons far too devastating. His exalted scientific status allowed him to state openly what others could not, including outside publication. He was not permitted to travel to Stockholm to receive the 1975 Nobel Prize for peace, and in 1980 was exiled to the closed city of Gorkiy, specifically to prevent contact with foreign journalists. Many regarded him as the conscience of the dissident movement.

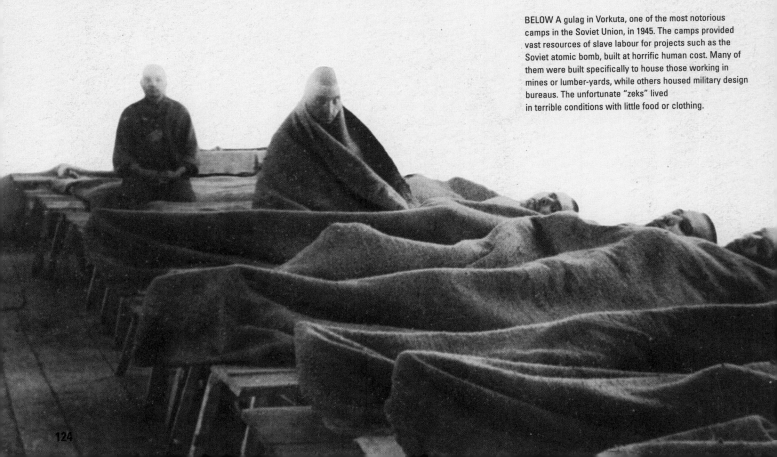

BELOW A gulag in Vorkuta, one of the most notorious camps in the Soviet Union, in 1945. The camps provided vast resources of slave labour for projects such as the Soviet atomic bomb, built at horrific human cost. Many of them were built specifically to house those working in mines or lumber-yards, while others housed military design bureaus. The unfortunate "zeks" lived in terrible conditions with little food or clothing.

ABOVE The KGB arrests a dissident, Alexander Podrabinek, during a Baptist prayer meeting in April 1977. Encouraged by the "human rights" clauses of the Helsinki Accord, he had led protests against the use of psychiatry to punish dissidents. Under the catch-all charge of "hooliganism" (which meant protesting), he was given a 15-day sentence.

CHAPTER 23

SOLIDARITY

The Soviet empire in Eastern Europe began in Poland at the end of World War II in 1945 and it began to end there three decades later.

By that time the limited economic reforms begun after the 1956 crisis were no longer working. In 1976 the Polish government tried to raise prices. A wave of strikes followed, and the Polish government gave ground. Uniquely in the Soviet bloc, the government was unable to crush the workers. In 1980 the government again raised prices. Workers in the shipbuilding centre of Gdansk went on strike. The yards there were a core Polish industry and, incidentally, a major resource for the Soviets (most Soviet amphibious ships came from Poland). The shipyard workers, led by Lech Wałęsa, formed a union, Solidarity,

to defend themselves. Given the fiction that Communist states were run by and for their workers, an independent union was inconceivable. The union seemed poised not only to gain control of a major Polish industry, but also to spread its influence through the country. Solidarity promised not merely to break open Poland itself but also to inspire a similar movement in the Soviet Union. Such unions were among the worst Soviet nightmares: they were independent centres of power that could effectively defy the Party. Even worse, in the Polish case, the intellectuals the Party considered

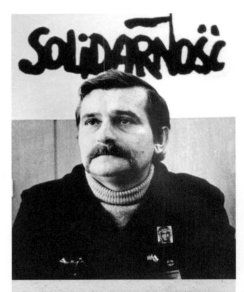

LECH WAŁĘSA (1943–)

Wałęsa created Solidarity, which brought down the Communist regime in Poland. In 1976 he became spokesman for demonstrators at a Gdańsk shipyard protesting the erosion of the settlement to the 1970 riots. Fired, he joined the underground Worker's Self-Defence Committee. When a strike broke out in Gdańsk in 1980 he climbed a wall to take charge of what became Solidarity. The martial law designed to break Solidarity convinced Wałęsa that no settlement within the Communist system was possible; he became Poland's first post-Communist president.

ABOVE Solidarity badge

RIGHT Solidarity badge for Gdansk '81

OPPOSITE The Polish Government declared martial law in the hopes of staving off a Soviet invasion to restore "socialist order".

1970
14 DECEMBER: RIOTS IN GDANSK AGAINST WAGE CUTS; GOMUŁKA RESIGNS

1976
25 JUNE: POLISH GOVERNMENT FORCED BY RIOTS TO WITHDRAW FOOD PRICE INCREASES

1978
16 OCTOBER: KAROL WOJTYŁA BECOMES POPE JOHN PAUL II

1980
14 AUGUST: STRIKE IN GDANSK; SOLIDARITY UNION FORMED

30 AUGUST: POLISH GOVERNMENT ALLOWS INDEPENDENT UNIONS; STRIKE ENDS

14 DECEMBER: NATO WARNS AGAINST SOVIET INVASION OF POLAND

1981
18 SEPTEMBER: SOVIETS DEMAND CRACKDOWN ON SOLIDARITY

13 DECEMBER: MARTIAL LAW DECLARED IN POLAND

1982
13 MARCH: SOLIDARITY, THOUGH BANNED, STAGES A LARGE-SCALE MARCH IN GDANSK

1989
25 JULY: HAVING WON ALL THE SEATS IT CONTESTED, SOLIDARITY REFUSES TO ENTER A COALITION WITH THE COMMUNISTS

24 AUGUST: POLISH COMMUNIST GOVERNMENT VOTED OUT OF OFFICE

BELOW The Polish government's nightmare began with the rise of the independent Solidarity union, initially at the Gdansk shipyard. Here its leader, Lech Wałęsa, speaks to his members during a strike, in August 1980.

its property became involved with the union.

The Roman Catholic Church in Poland was already a source of dissidence. The Communists instinctively attacked organized religion as a possible rival for power, but Poland was heavily Roman Catholic and Poles associated the Church with Polish nationalism. Until the late 1970s the Roman Catholic Church sought accommodation with the Communist government. There was little point in martyrdom if that would not change the government. In 1978 a Pole, Karol Wojtyła, was elected Pope John Paul II. He was a source of immense pride to Poles. Having lived under Nazi and Communist tyrannies, he refused to accept that Soviet rule would last forever. He sensed in Solidarity an opportunity for liberation. His Church supported Solidarity; some of its priests

preached Polish nationalism rather than obedience to the Party. In 1981 an un-successful attempt was made on the Pope's life in Rome; many believed the Soviets were desperately trying to eliminate a mortal threat to their empire.

Within months of the formation of Solidarity, a majority of the Soviet Politburo wanted to invade Poland. As in Afghanistan, the existing government was proving unable to handle a serious challenge: it could not destroy the union. However, by late 1980 the Afghan adventure seemed far less attractive. Marshal Ogarkov, chief of the Soviet general staff, doubted that the Soviet Union could support two such wars at the same time. Although the Politburo actually approved an invasion plan in November 1980,

Brezhnev backed off. Not only had he been warned off by the Americans, but it had become clear that the Poles would fight if they were invaded, given Polish hatred for the Russians and for the East Germans who would also have invaded. The Poles offered a solution: a military coup which would lead to martial law. The Minister of Defence, General Wojciech Jaruzelski, became Prime Minister in February 1981. By this time the combination of the Church and Solidarity was too strong to break. Through the 1980s Jaruzelski tried a combination of attacks and blandishments. As proof of his failure, in 1989 the Romanians tried to convince the other Warsaw Pact powers to invade Poland to break Solidarity, which had survived nearly a decade of Jaruzelski's attacks.

He was Polish Minister of Defence when the 1980 Solidarity crisis erupted. He was made Prime Minister in the hope that he could solve the problem without requiring Soviet military intervention. Then he was made head of the Party – an unprecedented seizure of power by the uniformed military in a Communist country. Accused of tyranny, Jaruzelski had defended himself as a Polish patriot, protecting the country from the Soviet invasion which would have been inevitable had Solidarity not been fought from inside the country.

BELOW Perhaps worse than the Solidarity problem, Polish-born Pope John Paul II was clearly the most popular man in the country. This is his visit to Warsaw in June 1979.

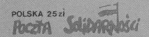

MĘCZENNICY I BOHATEROWIE DUCHOWNI

POLSKA 25 zł   Poczta Solidarności

POLSKA 30 zł   Poczta Solidarności

POLSKA 45 zł   Poczta Solidarności

POLSKA 50 zł   Poczta Solidarności

STANISŁAW BRZÓZKA
DOWÓDCA POWSTAŃCZY
ok.1834-1865

IGNACY SKORUPKA
KAPELAN WOJSKOWY
1893-1920

św. MAKSYMILIAN KOLBE
FRANCISZKAN
1894-1941

JERZY POPIEŁUSZKO
KAPELAN „SOLIDARNOŚCI"
1947-1984

ODDAŁ ŻYCIE
ZA SPRAWĘ NARODOWĄ

ODDAŁ ŻYCIE
ZA POLSKĘ

ODDAŁ ŻYCIE
ZA BRATA SWEGO

ODDAŁ ŻYCIE
ZA WIARĘ
I ZA OJCZYZNĘ

FUNDUSZ GRUP RKW NSZZ „S"

REGION MAZOWSZE   Solidarni

BELOW A Solidarity poster designed by Bielecki in 1980,
showing graphically the years in which the popular
pressure for freedom surged in Poland: 1944, '56, '68, '70,
'76 and '80.

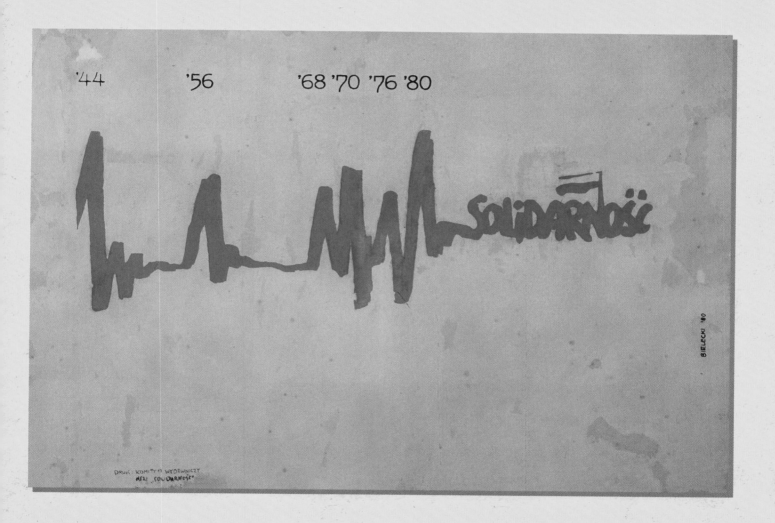

CHAPTER 24
PRESIDENT REAGAN'S OFFENSIVE

To many Americans, the Soviet invasion of Afghanistan proved that the Soviets were on the march. There was a strong sense that the United States had allowed itself to fall much too far behind.

In 1980 Americans elected Ronald Reagan on an aggressive Cold War platform. He called the Soviets "the evil Empire". That went directly against the accepted wisdom, in Europe and in many quarters in the United States, that the Soviet Union was a permanent if unpleasant fact of life, which it was quixotic to resist. The Cold War was inherently unwinnable, the goal of statesmanship being to develop an acceptable accommodation with that reality. The West ought not to embarrass the Soviets with which it had to live. Reagan, however, made it clear, for example, that he did not regard Poland as an internal Soviet matter. He helped make sure that

Poland would continue to be a running sore in the Soviet Empire. To those unaware that the Cold War had been fought in the 1960s and 1970s in places such as Vietnam and Africa, it seemed that Reagan had begun a new Cold War.

Reagan saw the Soviets as weak, not secure; vigorous policies might force them to abandon the Cold War altogether. Defence costs were hurting Western economies badly enough; surely astronomical costs hit the Soviets far worse. Unknown to Americans, by this time the Soviet economy was actually contracting while it was increasing defence spending, an unsupportable situation.

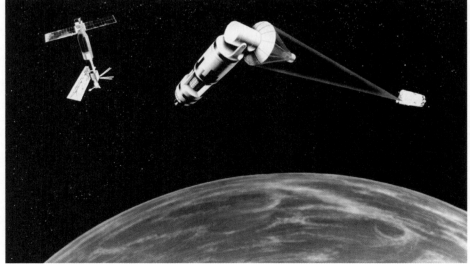

FAR LEFT President Reagan proclaimed a goal of eliminating offensive nuclear weapons, both by treaty and by developing US missile defences. Soviet attempts to copy the American "Star Wars" programme helped bankrupt them.

ABOVE In October 1983, US forces invaded the island of Grenada in the Caribbean, overthrowing its Cuban-oriented government. The invasion was intended to show Fidel Castro, seen as a Soviet proxy, that the

United States was willing to deal with him as well. Americans saw it as proof that the "Vietnam Syndrome" was finished.

BELOW Because Reagan's rearmament programme featured heavily computerized weapons like these F-15s, it helped dramatize the Soviet failure to develop a military computer industry. The urgent need to modernize Soviet industry forced Mikhail Gorbachev into his fatal liberalization.

Reagan's policies were designed to force the Soviets to spend even more on defence and so undermine their economy. He rebuilt American forces. Although he never said so, he seems to have justified the ruinous costs he ran on the grounds that they would end the Cold War altogether and so make it possible to cut defence spending in the long run – as actually happened. Very secret ("black") defence strategies were undertaken in hopes that their sudden disclosure would force the Soviets into crash programmes particularly destructive of their planned economy. Perhaps the most spectacular such programme was "Star Wars", the Strategic Defense Initiative (SDI) – an attempt to develop a defence against missile attack. Against the advice of Soviet scientists, the Soviet government sponsored an equivalent, the cost of which helped bankrupt it. It is still not clear to what extent, if any, the Reagan administration announced its programme with this end in mind.

Attacks on Soviet finances included making their loans more expensive and persuading the Saudis to cut the price of oil – since sales of Soviet oil were their major source of foreign exchange. Soviet oil production was declining as easily worked wells were exhausted. It would take more advanced – mainly American – technology to tap the much larger reserves still in the ground. President Reagan did his best to keep

1979
3 MAY: MARGARET THATCHER TAKES OFFICE

1981
20 JANUARY: RONALD REAGAN INAUGURATED AS PRESIDENT; FALKLANDS WAR BREAKS OUT

1982
9 DECEMBER: NATO FOREIGN MINISTERS VOTE TO ACCEPT US CRUISE AND PERSHING MISSILES

1983
25 OCTOBER: URGENT FURY – US FORCES ATTACK GRENADA

1985
11 MARCH: GORBACHEV TAKES OFFICE

19 NOVEMBER: GENEVA SUMMIT: GORBACHEV MEETS REAGAN (FIRST US-SOVIET SUMMIT SINCE 1979)

1987
22 JULY: GORBACHEV AGREES TO FIRST CUTS IN NUCLEAR WEAPONS (ABOLITION OF MEDIUM-RANGE WEAPONS)

1989
20 JANUARY: REAGAN LEAVES OFFICE

that out of Soviet hands. Reagan also tried to sabotage the Soviet project to sell piped natural gas to Western Europe, on the theory that the Europeans would come under Soviet control if they came to depend on Soviet gas for their energy.

Like Khrushchev, Reagan announced support for wars of national liberation – against the Soviets and their proxies. That included backing the Afghan guerrillas and also Africans and Nicaraguans fighting Cubans and their proxies.

Margaret Thatcher, whose views were somewhat similar to Reagan's, had recently become British Prime Minister. She shared the President's view that there was no point in appeasing the Soviets. They became close friends and allies, strongly agreeing on what had to be done to save the West. Overall, Mrs Thatcher championed a vigorous foreign policy. Although her fight in the Falklands was not part of the Cold War, it had a dramatic effect on the Soviets, showing that they had failed altogether to destroy British national spirit.

MARGARET THATCHER (1925–2013)

Thatcher became British Prime Minister in 1979 (the first woman premier in any major European country), remaining until 1990. She was instrumental in creating the decisive combination of keenness to "do business" with Mikhail Gorbachev without willingness to overlook Soviet misdeeds. Her decision to fight for the Falklands helped convince the Soviets that the West was not nearly so decadent as they had imagined. Her close relationship with US President Ronald Reagan was vital. Her success in reviving the British economy helped demonstrate that Capitalism had a future.

ABOVE To President Reagan, the global Soviet empire, including allies and proxy states, was fair game for American-sponsored pressure. When he entered office in 1981, a Cuban-backed regime was taking over Nicaragua. Contras, like the ones shown, were sponsored to attack them. When Congress refused to back the attacks, the National Security Council illegally used other funds to pay for the Contras' operations. An investigation failed to tie the scandal to the President. Ultimately the Nicaraguan regime collapsed.

OPPOSITE President Reagan deployed Tomahawk (like this one) and Pershing missiles in Europe to counter new Soviet missiles aimed at the Europeans. They were accurate enough to destroy Soviet command centres. The Soviets found to their surprise that they could not intimidate or cajole the Europeans into rejecting the weapons. Mikhail Gorbachev had to accept an agreement eliminating such weapons on both sides, the first time in the Cold War that nuclear arms were actually reduced.

CHAPTER 25

GORBACHEV: A MAN TO DO BUSINESS WITH

The Soviet Union entered the 1980s in crisis, its economy failing under the weight of enormous military programmes and Party incompetence.

Many Soviets had a sense that the country was in stagnation, that some change was badly needed. The elderly Leonid Brezhnev died in 1982, succeeded by the KGB's Yuri Andropov. Quite sick when he assumed power, Andropov died within two years, to be succeeded by the last of Brezhnev's generation, Konstantin Chernenko. He was clearly an interim choice, too sick to last long. Finally, in 1985 a man young enough to serve for years to come was chosen: Mikhail Gorbachev.

Gorbachev first met Ronald Reagan at Geneva in 1985, hoping to convince the President to cancel "Star Wars". Unfortunately he was not at all secure in his power – he needed the summit to prove his worth to the Politburo. The next year, at Reykjavik, Gorbachev tried to kill off the new intermediate-range missiles the United States was placing in Western Europe. Reagan extracted a ban on all such missiles on both sides. For the first time in the Cold War, an arms treaty, signed in 1987, actually reduced weapons on both sides. For Reagan, the lesson was clear: the only way to extract the desired cuts was to show determination in the face of Gorbachev's surprising weakness.

Gorbachev justified his election before the Politburo by promising to solve the crucial Soviet problem: military computer production. That was bound up with the larger Soviet economic problem.

Unlike Khrushchev (who had been ousted for doing so) Gorbachev could not simply order

OPPOSITE On the wrong side of the military balance, Mikhail Gorbachev had to smile at President Reagan while the President assaulted him at the US-Soviet summit held in Reykjavík in October 1986.

RIGHT One of Gorbachev's many problems was that now the Americans were sponsoring guerrillas to fight his troops and their proxies. These Contras are patrolling against the Cuban-backed Sandinistas in Nicaragua.

1982
10 NOVEMBER: BREZHNEV, LONG-TIME SOVIET LEADER, DIES

1984
9 FEBRUARY: YURI ANDROPOV, BREZHNEV'S SUCCESSOR, DIES

15 DECEMBER: GORBACHEV, POTENTIAL NEW SOVIET LEADER, VISITS BRITAIN

1985
10 MARCH: KONSTANTIN CHERNENKO, ANDROPOV'S SUCCESSOR, DIES

11 MARCH: GORBACHEV SELECTED AS NEXT SOVIET LEADER

23 APRIL: GORBACHEV ANNOUNCES PERESTROIKA (RESTRUCTURING)

16 MAY: GORBACHEV ANNOUNCES ANTI-DRINKING POLICIES

1986
25 FEBRUARY: GORBACHEV CALLS FOR RADICAL ECONOMIC REFORM

16 DECEMBER: ANDREI SAKHAROV RELEASED FROM INTERNAL EXILE

1989
26 MARCH: MULTI-PARTY ELECTION FOR SOVIET DUMA (PARLIAMENT)

ABOVE For the Soviet leadership, the disaster at Chernobyl in 1986 brought home for the first time in decades the reality of just how dangerous nuclear weapons could be. The reactor never exploded, but it did produce something like nuclear fallout, particularly in nearby areas. That ordinary Russians first learned of the disaster from Western sources emphasized the need for a more open Soviet society. Ukrainians later cited Chernobyl as evidence that they could not trust the Russians, and thus a reason for seeking independence (it also helped explain their decision to hand over all nuclear weapons on their soil to the Russians). Ruined Reactor No. 4 is seen from Reactor No. 3, both still giving off lethal levels of radiation.

plants turning out other things, such as tanks or aircraft, to produce computers instead. He had to convince a generation of very cynical Soviet workers to work much harder, and to expand the economy sufficiently to add new industries. It took a few years for Gorbachev to discover much of what Dubček had sensed almost immediately in Czechoslovakia, facing a similar problem almost 20 years earlier.

Slogans, the staple of Soviet management, were not enough: workers had heard too many of them for far too long. Nor did it do much good to ban drinking during working hours or to arrest workers who stayed out of work to queue to buy scarce goods. Gorbachev hit on two new ideas not too different from Dubček's: *glasnost* (openness) and *perestroika* (restructuring). He would carry out perestroika by unleashing the creativity of Soviet citizens, promising them they

would not be punished for speaking out of turn. The key guarantee was glasnost: truth, rather than Party cant, would be honoured. Like any other upper-level Party official, Gorbachev assumed that, given the chance, workers would concentrate on making the Soviet Union more successful. Given years of misrule, the subject of free expression was too often the crimes of the Party.

Nor could Gorbachev fall back on the traditional Soviet alternative, repression. On the wrong side of the military balance, he badly needed détente. Unlike their predecessors, neither President Reagan nor Mrs Thatcher saw much point in a détente which would merely be a breathing space before the Soviets became aggressive again. To them the only guarantee of peace was transformation inside the Soviet Union.

Gorbachev tried to outmanoeuvre his Western enemies by speaking directly to their populations, claiming (falsely) to cut military production and thus, in his words, undercutting them by removing the threat they cited. Although Gorbachev became popular in the West, this ploy failed.

Gorbachev gradually came to realize that the Party which had placed him in power was crippling the country. He therefore tried to cripple the Party, ending its monopoly on power. He never realized that the Party was also the sole mechanism which transmitted the ruler's orders to those who would carry them out. Without it, his new directives went nowhere. Stagnation was even worse than in Brezhnev's time. Gorbachev's tragedy was that he never understood his own political system well enough to develop any sort of viable replacement.

OPPOSITE US President Ronald Reagan meets the former USSR's General Secretary Mikhail Gorbachev at the first US–Russian summit.

RIGHT Gorbachev found himself freeing the dissidents and then being forced to accept them in a multi-party parliament, the Duma. Here the most famous dissident of all, Andrei Sakharov, addresses the Duma with Gorbachev looking on.

≡ MIKHAIL GORBACHEV (1931–)

Gorbachev had an unlikely background: his mentors were Yuri Andropov of the KGB and Mikhail Suslov, the reactionary ideologue of the Party. Both spent time in his district for kidney treatment. Once Andropov was in power, Gorbachev often acted as his deputy, but he was not the undisputed heir. Konstantin Ustinovich Chernenko was chosen as an interim leader, precisely because his short tenure would provide time for a longer-term choice. He was so feeble that Gorbachev often had to fill in for him, demonstrating his suitability as leader.

BELOW For Mikhail Gorbachev, the key problem was to overcome the ingrained Soviet instinct to avoid any kind of active participation in the system, except for entirely careerist motives, and at the behest of a hidebound Communist Party. He hoped that opening politics – in a controlled way – would help solve the problem, to get his country moving. The elected multi-party Duma, which he is shown addressing, was one way of doing that. What Gorbachev never expected was that once he opened politics, his own position would come into question, and that his policies might be rejected. As the creature of a dictatorial system, he was poorly equipped for open politics.

BELOW AND OPPOSITE Soviet posters from the era of *glasnost* and *perestroika*. One reads, "Got the wings, then move further!", celebrating new freedoms of the press; the other, "The local office of the Young Communist League is closed because all members are on the Perestroika front."

THE WALL COMES DOWN

The war in Afghanistan and the ongoing political crisis in Poland seem to have convinced Mikhail Gorbachev that the East European empire could no longer be held by force.

In 1988 he announced what became known as the "Sinatra Doctrine," named (in 1989) after the singer's signature song: "I'll do it my way." Never again would the Soviet Union impose its form of Communism on an Eastern European country by force. The Communist leaders of Eastern Europe vehemently disagreed, but Gorbachev had the troops. Now they were doomed, and they knew it. Gorbachev did not realize how devastating his decision was. He imagined that 40 years of Communist rule had produced a reasonably content population which would welcome a more relaxed version of Communism. Nor could he imagine just how vivid memories of Russian crimes, such as the suppression of Hungary in 1956 and the massacre

of Poles at Katyn in 1940, were throughout Eastern Europe.

Hungary, led by Károly Grósz, was already the least conservative of the satellite countries. Given the "Sinatra Doctrine", in the summer of 1989 it decided to open its border to the West. Many Hungarians already travelled back and forth across the border, for example to trade in Austria. The radical step was that non-Hungarians might also cross. That in effect destroyed the Iron Curtain, because travel within the Communist bloc was relatively easy. That was acceptable only because the bloc as a whole was closed to the West. Letting East Germans through would destroy the East German regime: it would be like going back to the situation before the Wall.

ERICH HONECKER (1912–1994)

Honecker replaced Walter Ulbricht because he accepted the West German opening to the East (Ostpolitik), which the Soviets considered useful. That required greater repression in East Germany; otherwise the population might come to expect freedom. In 1980 Honecker demanded a Czech-style invasion to put down the Polish Solidarity movement. In 1988 he rejected glasnost and perestroika. By the time Mikhail Gorbachev was visiting him for the 40th anniversary of East Germany, a coup to unseat him was already well advanced.

1989

6 MARCH: SOVIETS RENOUNCED BREZHNEV DOCTRINE IN FAVOUR OF "SINATRA DOCTRINE"

AUGUST: CEAUŞESCU OF ROMANIA DEMANDS THAT WARSAW PACT INVADE POLAND TO CRUSH SOLIDARITY

2 MAY: HUNGARIANS BEGIN OPENING THEIR BORDER TO AUSTRIA

10 SEPTEMBER: EAST GERMAN NEUES FORUM ORGANIZATION FORMED IN EAST BERLIN

11 SEPTEMBER: FIRST 10,000 EAST GERMANS ARRIVE IN WEST GERMANY VIA HUNGARY

7 OCTOBER: GORBACHEV VISITS EAST GERMANY

18 OCTOBER: EAST GERMAN COUP: HONECKER REPLACED BY EGON KRENZ

4 NOVEMBER: EAST GERMANY'S BIGGEST DEMONSTRATION: ONE MILLION IN EAST BERLIN

9 NOVEMBER: EAST GERMAN BORDERS OPENED; THE WALL FALLS AS GUARDS STAND BY

28 NOVEMBER: WEST GERMAN CHANCELLOR HELMUT KOHL ANNOUNCES REUNIFICATION PLAN

OPPOSITE Mikhail Gorbachev and his East European enemies occupy the front row at the 40th anniversary celebration of East Germany, on 7 October 1989. Left to right: Wojciech Jaruzelski of Poland,

Milouš Jakeš of Czechoslovakia, Gorbachev, Erich Honecker of East Germany. Out of shot to the left is Nicolae Ceauşescu of Romania. By the year's end only Gorbachev was left.

ABOVE With Erich Honecker ousted, and the "Sinatra Doctrine" in place, East Germans were suddenly able to rally against their government. This crowd is in Leipzig, a centre of German dissent.

When the Hungarians asked Russian permission, they were told that, in accord with the new doctrine, what they did with their border was their own business.

Probably Gorbachev was pleased, because he feared that the remaining conservative rulers of Eastern Europe would provide havens for those Russians intent on overthrowing him. The most diehard of them all was Erich Honecker of East Germany. Visiting East Germany for the 40th anniversary of the state, Gorbachev publicly attacked Honecker for his unwillingness to reform. Sensing an opening, East Germans demonstrated in East Berlin, Dresden, Leipzig and other cities. Their Neues Forum organization had been formed about a month earlier in East Berlin. At first the Stasi attacked the crowds, but

not hard enough to suppress the movement. By this time the East German economy was in crisis as a consequence of the mass exodus through Hungary. These problems were used to justify what amounted to a Stasi coup against Honecker, who was replaced by the Stasi chief, Egon Krenz. Now the Stasi stood back, and a million people demonstrated in East Berlin. Even so, Gorbachev thought that the East German regime would continue as before. He imagined that ultimately a "liberalized" East Germany might join a confederation with West Germany, finally neutralizing that country.

Taking power, the new rulers suddenly discovered that East Germany was broke. Gorbachev had no hard currency to offer them, so they went to the West Germans, in the past

always willing to provide enough to keep East Germany going. This time the West German Chancellor Helmut Kohl asked for moderate reforms such as easier terms for families in East Germany to rejoin their relatives in the West. The new East German government panicked: it officially gave up the Communist Party's monopoly on power. It also opened the Berlin Wall. With world media watching, an ecstatic crowd began to smash down the Wall. Kohl immediately put a reunification plan before the West German Bundestag. He soon manoeuvred Gorbachev into approving unification on his terms, Germany remaining in NATO. To the extent that the Cold War had been about the fate of Germany, Gorbachev had lost.

ABOVE Symbolic of all the East German regime feared and tried to suppress, an East German punk helps destroy the Wall on 10 November 1989, the day after it fell.

OPPOSITE The Wall is dead: Berliners, who can now be united, sit atop the Berlin Wall in front of the Brandenburg Gate, the symbol of their city.

CHAPTER 27
REVOLUTIONS IN EASTERN EUROPE

To the orthodox Communist rulers of Eastern Europe, Poland was a running sore. Jaruzelski's failure to crush Solidarity endangered all of them.

In Hungary the government declared that in 1956 the Soviets had not put down a counter-revolution but, on the contrary, had crushed a legitimate government. In July 1989 Gorbachev shocked a Warsaw Pact meeting by supporting the Poles and the Hungarians. That August, Nicolae Ceauşescu of Romania demanded that the Pact invade Poland to crush Solidarity; he thought it was 1968 and that Poland was Czechoslovakia. Gorbachev, however, was not Brezhnev. The Poles were so contemptuous that they published Ceauşescu's letter.

Demonstrations alone probably would not have overthrown the remaining orthodox Communist governments. They still had powerful secret police and they had their own armies. Gorbachev, however, still feared that his Russian enemies would find refuges in the hard-line countries of Eastern Europe – which he now viewed as a net burden rather than an invaluable asset. Given his background working with the Soviet secret police, he had close ties with the secret police of the other Warsaw Pact countries, even those of the semi-estranged Romania.

Mass demonstrations began in Czechoslovakia a few days after the Wall collapsed in Berlin. Not only did the police not break them up, they seem to have encouraged them. The demonstrations were used within the Czechoslovak Party to justify a change of leadership. Gorbachev's intent was probably simply to replace the existing hardline regime with a softer one, but the Czechoslovak population was having none of that. The Communist regime quickly yielded power to Václav Havel, who had long been a leader of the dissident Charter 77 movement.

Events at the end of 1989 in Romania were far more dramatic. Ceauşescu was the most obdurate of the Communist dictators. He was so intent on maintaining power that he forced all owners of typewriters to register samples of

VÁCLAV HAVEL (1936–2011)

Havel was an absurdist playwright and philosopher before becoming involved in the Charter 77 movement. He was already in trouble for his unconventional writings, and given his continued underground activities he was imprisoned from time to time for his writings. His growing fame outside Czechoslovakia helped limit the sentences. Thus, sentenced to nine months in February 1989, he was released after four. He led in the formation of the Civic Forum opposition group which replaced the Communist government of Czechoslovakia, and in January 1990 was chosen President.

ABOVE Havel supporters' badge

EASTERN EUROPE 1989–90

Communists states, mid-1989

Communists government dissolved, with date

Yugoslavia, 1990

EAST GERMANY
Oct–Nov 1989 demonstrations against leadership
9 Nov 1989 Berlin Wall breached
Oct 1990 Reunification with West Germany

Baltic Sea
Gdansk
Vilnius

P O L A N D
Warsaw
Jan 1990
Wroclaw
Kraków

U N I O N
Minsk
O F   S O V I E T
Kiev
S O C I A L I S T
Lvov
R E P U B L I C S

WEST GERMANY
Bonn
Leipzig
BEL.
Frankfurt
GERMANY

FRANCE
Munich
Rhine
Danube
SWITZERLAND

C Z E C H O S L O V A K I A
Prague

A U S T R I A
Vienna
Budapest
H U N G A R Y
Nov 1989
Oct 1990

SLOVENIA
Zagreb
C R O A T I A
Belgrade

R O M A N I A
Communist leader Nikolai Ceauşescu executed, Dec 1989
Communists remain in power
Bucharest
Danube

Kishinev
Odessa
Dnieper

Black Sea

I T A L Y
Rome
Corsica
Sardinia

Y U G O S L A V I A
Tension between Communist government and Croatia and Slovenia

B U L G A R I A
Sofia
Dec 1989
Burgas

Tirana
A L B A N I A
Democratic reforms lead to free elections in Mar 1991

Istanbul

Salonika
G R E E C E
T U R K E Y

BELOW A Romanian civilian chases security forces loyal to President Ceauşescu. It now appears that all or most of the civilians involved were actually members of security forces loyal to Ion Iliescu, Ceauşescu's successor, and it was probably not a popular rebellion.

1989

11 JANUARY: HUNGARIAN GOVERNMENT COMMISSION REVERSES OFFICIAL CLAIM THAT THE 1956 REVOLUTION WAS A FOREIGN OPERATION

18 FEBRUARY: POLISH GOVERNMENT ADMITS THAT SOVIETS, NOT GERMANS, CARRIED OUT THE KATYN FOREST MASSACRE

17 MARCH: HUGE HUNGARIAN DEMONSTRATIONS RECALL 1848 RISING; PROTEST AGAINST COMMUNIST GOVERNMENT

16 JUNE: IMRE NAGY REBURIED WITH HONOURS: THE HUNGARIAN REVOLUTION ITSELF IS HONOURED

7 OCTOBER: HUNGARIAN COMMUNIST PARTY ABANDONS LENINISM

28 OCTOBER: MASS DEMONSTRATIONS IN PRAGUE CRUSHED BY POLICE

17 NOVEMBER: POLICE ATTACK RENEWED DEMONSTRATIONS IN PRAGUE

24 NOVEMBER: CZECHOSLOVAK COMMUNIST GOVERNMENT RESIGNS

24 NOVEMBER: ROMANIAN PRESIDENT NICOLAE CEAUŞESCU CONFIRMED IN OFFICE

25 DECEMBER: ROMANIAN PRESIDENT NICOLAE CEAUŞESCU AND HIS WIFE ARE EXECUTED

their output, so that any dissident letters could be traced to their authors! As in the other satellite states, the crisis began with huge demonstrations, triggered, in this case, by rumours. His own secret police brought Ceauşescu down, and, uniquely in the bloc, he and his wife were executed. This was more like what Gorbachev had in mind, in that the successor regime was really another Communist group (albeit nominally non-Communist). It lasted several more years.

Within a few months the empire Stalin had erected in Eastern Europe had crumbled. The people of countries absorbed into the Soviet Union itself still wanted out. Foremost among them were the three Baltic republics – Estonia, Latvia and Lithuania – which had been brought forcibly into the Soviet Union in 1940 as a result of the secret clauses of the treaty between Hitler and Stalin – clauses the existence of which the

Soviet state had always denied (it claimed accession had been voluntary). Once the Communist Party gave up its statutory dominance, people in the Baltic states were free to elect parliaments which reflected their own desire for independence. For his part, Gorbachev found himself compelled to admit that Stalin's crimes had included seizing the three republics. Nevertheless, Gorbachev denounced declarations of independence by the Baltic states' parliaments, and sent in some troops. For example, in January 1991 they seized the television station in Vilnius, Lithuania, killing 13 people. However, Gorbachev could not afford full-scale suppression in the Baltic states, because he could not afford the rupture with the West that such action would have caused. The three Baltic republics were allowed to secede. It was up to Gorbachev to convince the elected governments of the other republics not to follow suit.

ABOVE Victory: a Romanian flag, with the Communist red star cut out of it, is waved in Bucharest, in December 1989.

RIGHT Only in Romania did the handover of power involve violence. It now appears that the former Romanian President Ion Iliescu carried out a coup, which some secret police loyal to Nicolae Ceauşescu resisted. Here soldiers and anti-Communist civilians gather in front of the destroyed library in Bucharest.

RIGHT Václav Havel
election poster which
reads, "Havel for the
Castle". This meant "Havel
for President", as the
Castle in Prague was the
official residence of the
Czech President.

HAVEL NA HRAD

CHAPTER 28

FALL OF THE SOVIET UNION

Gorbachev never saw himself as another Dubček. He thought that he was reforming the Soviet Union to save it, not sink it. Among his reforms were multi-candidate elections in the different republics making up the Soviet Union.

In some of them nationalists looked to the Baltic states and thought about their own full independence. Others were quite willing to remain in the Soviet Union, so long as they gained a measure of independence from Moscow. To Gorbachev, the solution was to turn the Soviet Union into a confederation bound by a new treaty.

To Gorbachev's enemies, the proposed treaty was the last straw. It had taken a remarkably long time for them to realize that, intentionally or not, Mikhail Gorbachev was destroying the system which had given them power. In August 1991 Gorbachev went on holiday by the Black Sea, planning to return to sign the treaty. His enemies deposed him in a coup led by Vice President Gennady I. Yanayev. The coup foundered, partly due to the courage shown by Boris Yeltsin, who had been elected President of the Russian Republic (within the Soviet Union). Yeltsin suddenly realized that he actually had greater legitimacy than Gorbachev, because he had actually been elected by popular vote, whereas Gorbachev had merely been appointed by the Communist Party's Politburo. It was Yeltsin who declared the coup illegal and then held out in Moscow, inside the Russian Republic parliament building (the so-called White House), and harangued besieging troops at their tanks.

Gorbachev was brought back into power — though a much-reduced power because of Yeltsin's rise. Yeltsin demanded that the Communist Party, which had organized the coup,

150

OPPOSITE To Yeltsin, the problem was, and had always been, the Party; despite the coup, Gorbachev thought that the Soviet Communist Party could still solve the country's problems. Here Yeltsin demands that Gorbachev resign as General Secretary of the Party, the post that previous Soviet rulers since Stalin had occupied.

THE DISSOLUTION OF THE USSR 1991

— Soviet Union at dissolution

▮ Commonwealth of Independent States that gained independence from USSR

▮ Other states that gained independence from USSR

— Constituent republics of Russian Federation

be declared illegal. Gorbachev tried to negotiate a new treaty of union, but he failed. Among other problems, the Ukrainians did not want to be part of the same Soviet Union which had produced the Chernobyl nuclear accident and which, within living memory, had presided over mass killings and starvations in Ukraine in the 1930s. Without the treaty, the Soviet Union was dissolved in December 1991. A new Confederation of Independent States, including all of the former Soviet republics except for the three Baltic states, was created; the Russians tried to maintain control of defence and foreign affairs. In practice that attempt failed, and the different republics ultimately followed their own policies, much to the anger of many Russians.

With the breakup of the Soviet Union, the Cold War was finally over. The pressures the Soviet system had generated had been far too much for it; the one man who had tried to solve the system's problems had been unable to see beyond it to something viable.

The many consequences of the Cold War live on. Europe (at least outside Russia) is, as Ronald Reagan used to say, "whole and free", the former Soviet imperial states are now either in or about to join NATO and the European Union. That is a vast achievement. Whatever horrors terrorism by fundamentalists currently holds, with the end of the Cold War there is no longer a sense anywhere in the West that a thousand nuclear missiles can be launched on a dictator's whim. The world is no longer, at least for now, on the brink of destruction.

However, the end of the Cold War has not ended the passions and ambitions that brought it about. The current Russian government would still like to regain some of the power it lost when its empire collapsed. Many of the former subjects of that empire are still resisting their pressures. The fight over the Ukrainian election of 2004 was only one of a long series of episodes. Russian troops are still fighting in what used to be Soviet

Central Asia, among other things to protect the large Russian ethnic populations left there. Similarly, many in Moscow were furious when the three Baltic states joined NATO, bringing the old Cold War border onto their own territory.

There have been many indirect consequences, too. Yugoslavia disintegrated into war in the 1990s in large part because, with the collapse of the Soviet Union, there was no longer an external threat to hold that country together. The rebel success in Afghanistan undoubtedly convinced many in the Muslim world that Allah had blessed their movement, with consequences we see around us almost every day. The Cold War has ended. The War on Terrorism has begun.

BORIS YELTSIN (1931–2007)

Yeltsin learned just how exciting democracy could be when he began winning elections after Mikhail Gorbachev ejected him from a Party Central Committee position in 1987. He soon realized that elections gave him a legitimacy the Party – and Mikhail Gorbachev – lacked. As elected president of the Russian Federation (within the Soviet Union), he resisted the 1991 coup from within the Russian Federation building (the "White House") in Moscow, facing down the threat of attack by special forces. Later he demanded that the Communist Party, responsible for the coup, be banned.

BELOW Russian leader doll set, from Lenin to Yeltsin

ABOVE By 1991 the Soviet Union had changed. When Mikhail Gorbachev's enemies staged a coup, the people of Moscow resisted, and the troops refused simply to run them down.

TRANSLATIONS

Page 15: Anti-Communist propaganda leaflet *The Truth*, published in 1953 by the West German Volksbund für Frieden und Freiheit (VFF).

[Front cover]
The Truth

Albania
Hungary
Bulgaria
Soviet Zone and East German Zone
Czechoslovakia
Romania
Poland
Korea

[Page 4]
We want Germans in the East and West to sit around the table of democracy, freedom and human dignity.
We want Germany to achieve peace, but a peace that includes freedom, security and independence.
We want Germany to be reunited, but without the SED, without Communist joy, without the collective, and without terror.

We want a Germany that is united and free!

[Cartoon]
I said "Unity"!

Soviet Zone
West Germany
France

[Page 5]
"All Germans at the same table"

This is what Stalin wants

The entire German People are asked to take the decision into their own hands and to accomplish German unity and freedom

This is what we want

Page 15: Early Communist propaganda brochure with a moral tale in rhyme.

[Front]
Uphill or downhill, now that is the question,
The answer, my friend, is up to you.
If you choose uphill then congratulations,
You have chosen the right thing to do.

Statewide price slumps due to sales crisis!
Full of cunning, their aim to besmirch –
 RIAS [Radio In the American Sector] is whispering lies in your ear.

RIAS

Statewide price drops due to successful completion of production goals!
Berlin State Radio will tell you no lie,

Your hard work has paid off: living standards are high!

Berlin State Radio

Step 1

Telegraph reading room

Read the *Telegraph* and you're well on your way,
To helping the saboteurs win the day.

Reference book collection. Advance through learning!

Learning will quickly help your rise,
So start it early, if you're wise.

Step 2

"10 parts you brought me were no good"
"I thought I did the best I could!"

"I worked even harder and planned ahead
and made ten parts more than my quota said."

Step 3

[Wall poster]
Maximum prices for non-ferrous metals:
 Brass…Westmark
 Tin…Westmark
 Lead…Westmark
 Copper…Westmark

Listening to RIAS has brought him down this way
– For this theft he will have to pay.

[Wall sign]
Cash office. Collect your wages and salary here.

"You've exceeded your norms – you've made a killing!
Your pay packet is in danger of spilling!"

Step 4

Please turn over.

[Back]
After these first four steps, now stop and think,
Is it better to rise, or better to sink?
One man in his own strength believed –
And as a result great things achieved.

The other listened to RIAS and its lies,
And is now faced with his own demise.
He chose the path that was heading down,
Now who is the wise man, and who the clown?

[Sign]
Task force against humanity

"You too can go round in clothes like these,
But first, let me tell you a story, please."

Hard work, good pay and you're well en route
To a rendezvous with a brand new suit.

[HO on shop tags stands for state-produced products]
Step 5

 "Now, young man, where shall I begin,
What story should I tell to drag you in?
Let's make a bang, and ensure that sparks fly!
Big deal if a couple of Germans die."

"Reports and figures, my dear man!
We are still not doing the best that we can!
Help us, my friend, to make production soar,
So that we can live better than ever before!"

[Wall poster]
Work voluntarily undertaken

[Paper in man's hand]
Experience report from 1950…

Step 6

Step 7

Listening to RIAS is where this began,
And now it has gone as far as it can.
His freedom will now be taken away,
He will live behind bars, full of dismay.

It all began with an eagerness to learn,
The will to improve his only concern.
And the end of his rise is still not in sight,
He will move on. His future is bright.

[Door sign]
General Management

Step 8

Page 25: Yankee Beetles: Stop! East German propaganda leaflet alleging that the Berlin Airlift was a cover for American airdrops of Colorado beetles to ruin East German Crops.

[Front cover]
YANKEE BEETLES

STOP!

[Pages 2–3]
In an expression of protest, the German and foreign journalists reported that:

 "The unanimous reports from the farmers who have experienced this affliction in their fields confirm the fact that huge numbers of Colorado beetles were found the day after American planes flew over the area.
 Colorado beetles are smaller than atom bombs, but they are another American imperialist weapon against the peace-

loving and hard-working population.

We, as journalists, aim to serve freedom, and we hereby strongly condemn this new and criminal tactic of the American warmongers."

This statement of protest carried the following signatures: Wu Wen Tao ("New China" agency), Ryszard Szymanski (API Poland), Kamila Cwylenska (Freedom Tribune, Poland), Victor Schleß (Czechoslovakian Press Office), Arrigo Jacchia (Il Paese, Rome), Lydia Lambert (Paris). All the participating German journalists also added their signatures.

The farmers assured the journalists that the discovery could have no other explanation other than the fact that the American planes seen in the area dropped the beetles. Colorado beetles normally first appear in mid-July, but this year they were found at the end of May. If the beetles had developed from larvae, there would have been much evidence of this because damage caused by the larvae feeding would have been noticeable. There was, however, no such evidence on the leaves of the potato plants. In the previous year, four Colorado beetles had been found in this area. This year 1,300 have been discovered. The farmers noticed, in particular, that the Colorado beetles found were of exactly the same size. This indicates that the beetles were bred.

Whereas it was once the Germans and the Japanese and their total war of extermination that threatened the world, we are now in danger from this evil gangster diplomacy. This booklet will provide unquestionable proof of this fact and expose the true face of the deadly enemy of mankind and peace for all men.

The current American government is trying to silence those campaigning for social progress and for peace in their own land by using the most brutal, fascist and violent methods. The same government intends to force the whole world under the rule of Dollar imperialism by using atom bombs and bacteria as deterrents. The decision-makers within the American government, and its mercenaries and henchmen who gather around the traitor Adenauer and his breakaway government in Bonn should be tried as war criminals. This is the just wish of the German farmers, and, along with them, all the advocates for peace and progress throughout the world.

Colorado beetles dropped by American planes

Report from the GDR Government Commission for the Investigation of Unusual Incidents

In a meeting of the Council of Ministers of the GDR government on 15 June 1950, the Secretary of State for Agriculture and Forestry reported that…

[Illustration]
The Colorado beetle under the magnifying glass.

A sketch by the famous Soviet caricaturist Kukrinski

Page 52: Declaration of a State of Emergency on 17 June 1953 by the Military Commander of the Soviet Sector of Berlin.

An Order

From the Military Commander of the Soviet Sector of Berlin

It concerns: Declaration of a State of Emergency in the Soviet Sector of Berlin

In order to establish secure public order in the Soviet Sector of

Berlin, the following has been ordered:

1. From 1300 on the 17th June 1953, a State of Emergency has been declared in the Soviet Sector of Berlin.
2. All demonstrations, meetings, rallies and other gatherings of three people or more in the streets and squares and in public buildings shall be banned.
3. All pedestrian traffic, heavy vehicle and private vehicle traffic shall be banned between the hours of 9pm and 5am.
4. Those breaking this order shall be punished according to wartime law.

The Military Commander of the Soviet Sector of Berlin

Major General

BIBROWA

Berlin, 17th June 1953

Page 53: Special issue of the satirical monthly *Tarantel* (Tarantula), covering the uprising in East Berlin.

[Front cover]
Tarantel: The Soviet zone's satirical monthly magazine.

Price: priceless

Special issue

[Cartoon, top left]
Government of the GDR

Patient passes away

When the most immortal of the wise immortals passed away at the beginning of spring, who would have thought that his changeling, the GDR, would follow him to the grave so quickly? The same hands who handed over our clocks and our harvests, the whole of Eastern Germany, and the skills of the German prisoners of war into the care of our Soviet friends have now also handed them governmental power. Our GDR is now as dead and buried as its heavily moustached founder. After a successful operation by Soviet tanks, the patient is now dead. The fat cats in the Government can be thankful for this sacrifice, because they can now bask their grief-wracked bodies in the warmth of the Moscow sun for a while longer. Before High Commissioner Semyonov gathers together a better set of qualified traitors to try and repeat Mitschurin's experiment of creating a Soviet-German cross-breed, the old dogs can feed on Soviet charity at the wailing wall in Karlshorst. Who would begrudge Semyonov this task? He wants to get hold of another twelve vultures, but instead of this, 18 million Germans are clamouring around his neck.

The medicine with which Moscow intended to heal the gallstone of German resistance has proved to be a feeble treatment. It will not even be enough to send the Officials for a healing course at Comrade Kruglow's spa. Working together, the German farmers and workers will make a sacrifice of them, as they did the last three dozen Vopo members and Government officials who wanted to prolong their history by using the barrel of a gun. They will learn too late and hang because of it.

The announcement that there would be no more power cuts in the third quadrant should not have been necessary. When it comes to taking care of the Germans, the lights went out long ago.

[Box text]

"When a free nation is faced with ruin due to the actions of the government, then it is not merely right for a member of the people to rebel, it is a duty!" – J.W.Stalin 8. 9. 42

German-Soviet Friendship!

Farmers! Have you handed your complete harvest over to the state? Every ear of corn is a contribution to German-Soviet friendship!

Rail workers! Are you working hard to repay all reparations on time? Every rail carriage sends a message of German-Soviet friendship!

Miners! Have you signed yourself up for voluntary extra shifts? Every ton of ore that you supply strengthens German-Soviet friendship!

Workers! Despite equipment shortages, have you managed to complete all your piecework without mistakes? Think about this: every defective item threatens German-Soviet friendship!

Officials! Are you watchful and do you report all suspicious people to the police? Even this is an expression of German-Soviet friendship!

All those fit for work! Do you see the Soviet tanks on our streets? Even they are tools for German-Soviet friendship!

[Cartoon, centre]
The little official

MODEST

"Inflammatory elements have used your discontent for their own gain," said Walter Ulbricht today, speaking to a group of workers in the East sector of Berlin. "But the decisions of the Central Committee will improve things. I promise you a reduction in working norms and a reduction in rail tariffs."

"Don't bother," interrupted a worker, "we have already had enough of Government promises."

After 17 June

Comrades! Don't be so sad!
Climb back out of your hole!
The GDR may now be merely symbolic,
But the Soviet tanks are still real!

WORDS OF AKNOWLEDGEMENT

"We must acknowledge that the discipline of the Soviet troops has greatly improved since 1945. In 1945 they raped hundreds of thousands of German women. In June 1953, they only raped the Constitution."

UNGRATEFUL

"See, Comrade General," said Ulbricht to a visitor to the GDR, "how unpredictable the people can be. In 1948, I promised the workers a noticeable improvement in their economic situation, and everything was fine. I made the same promise in 1949 and again in 1950. I swore the same in 1951 and 1952, and yet when I repeated the promise in 1953, they suddenly started to demonstrate!"

WHY CHANGE DIRECTION?

"When you are bitten by a mosquito, you should kill it. When an elephant stands on your foot, you should ask him for forgiveness."
CONFUCIUS
(Chinese philosopher, 551–478 BC)

[Cartoon, bottom]
Wheels must turn for victory!

[Footer]
If it takes a long time to cook, the result will be good

A NEW RUSSIAN PHRASE BOOK

With the takeover of governmental power by our Soviet friends, the SED and the Central Committee, along with the Marx-Engels-Stalin-Institute in Moscow, have prepared a revised edition of the **"Pocket Handbook for German-Soviet Language"** The errors in the previous edition have also been corrected. The following examples have been taken from the new edition, and clearly reflect the change of circumstances:

"Dawei, dawei!"	= "Please take your time!"
"Ruki wjerch!"	= "Do you need a light, comrade?"
"Rabota, rabota!"	= "Please make yourself comfortable."
"Dawei wodka!"	= "Can I offer you a glass of schnapps?"
"Uri, uri!"	= "Excuse me, what is the time?"
"Frau, ssjuda!"	= "Pleased to meet you, madam."
"Dokument nix charascho!"	= "Take a look in the Constitution yourself."
"MWD"	= "Always at your service!"
"Tschistka"	= "A favourite Russian parlour game, invented by Lomonossow."
"Katorga"	= "Recreational activities"
"Ntaschalnik"	= "My dear friend!"
"Njet"	= "Please, after you!"

PEOPLE – PLANTS – ANIMALS

"We have made some mistakes," said Grotewohl, "but we have also had successes!" –
"There are no roses without thorns," said the cactus, referring to its thorny skin.

*

"The Party and the working classes must work together!" says the Central Committee.
"Well, how can I get away from you then!" exclaimed the burr, as it clung to the horse's tail.

*

"The Government will not consider retreating in a cowardly manner!" said Grotewohl to the workers at Borsig.
"When you are in power, you are in the right!" thought the mistletoe, as it sucked the life from the apple tree.

[Top right poster]
The bunker for Government Officials
[Label on bear]
Gathering place for Government Officials
[Caption]
Throughout the time of Western provocation, the Germans and the Soviets maintained their friendship.

[Caption, column 1]
"Comrades! On the 17 June we stood side-by-side with our population for the first time!"

ONWARDS, ONWARDS!

Children, we thought it would be like this:
500 days – gone amiss!
500 songs – all of them rhyming!
500 speakers – all of them chiming!
Norms and medals – down the pan!
Long live the wonderful five-year plan!

OBITUARY

Beside the grave of the peacefully entombed SSD Chief Rathenower, hanged by the workers, a plaque was found today. It read: "This man was paid twice for the same job. He spied on us for years, and earned a thick pay packet from the Government for his services. On 17 June, he got his payment from us."

Exemplary as always

How often have we carried around banners with the slogans "Pull back the occupation troops now!" The agitators told us that our Soviet friends would be the first to pull back if it ever came to it. Nobody believed that. But we should have! 17 June proved that. We saw Soviet troops taking up positions, their fingers pulling back on the trigger. So that was that: the Soviets were the only occupying power to ever pull back. And we Germans will never forget it!

Questions from a Worker who Reads

(BASED ON A POEM BY BERT BRECHT)
What happened on 17 June?
In the politburo you will hear them talk of "some agitators".
Did the agitators open fire on the workers?
And what about "the agents from a foreign power"?
Who provoked the foreign tanks?
In which of the four sectors
Of divided Berlin
Did the construction workers strike?
Where did our Government workers hide?
For at last there was Government work to be done.
The entire land under marshal law.
Over whom did the T-34s triumph.
Did the workers' Fatherland only
Have tanks for sons? Even from
Behind their barricades
In the Government offices,
The powers that be,
Were afraid for their people.
The politburo can be self-critical.
Nothing more?
10 Marks more for your pension.
Could Chemnitz not have become Chemnitz again?
Ulbricht and Grotewohl believe,
That they have escaped again.
Does anybody still believe that?
They say they have learnt
From what has happened.
What will Moscow learn?
Every day a promise.
Who still believes that?
A long list of admitted failures.
When will the bill be paid?
So many reports, – So many questions

[Cartoon, columns 1–2]
[Banner in both pictures]
Walter Ulbricht speaks
[Cartoon caption]
"Self-criticism can be practised by beating the chest hard"

[Footer]
If you push too hard, it is you who will break

Page 57: A flyer distributed during the Hungarian Uprising by the University Student Revolutionary Committee.

"OUR TRUST IS IN IMRE NAGY"

This was still the slogan on Tuesday, 23 October.

This trust has become a little weaker over the past two or three days, but it is now stronger than ever!

It was revealed that Imre Nagy had been a **prisoner of the ÁVÓ for two days.** He made his first speech on the radio with a machine-gun held to his back.

It has become clear from his latest speech that it was not he who had ordered martial law and the intervention of the Soviet troops. Criminals like Rákosi and Gerő made up these cruel rumours in order to overturn him.

We, therefore, place our trust in you, Imre Nagy.

We do, however, warn you to safeguard the trust of the nation! You must immediately distance yourself from the traitors to our country!
You must immediately clean up the government and remove the old leftover rubbish, rightfully despised and hated by our nation.

You must organize the withdrawal of the Soviet troops from the country!
You must make sure that the ÁVÓ-members cannot infiltrate the new police force!
Imre Nagy's willingness to take responsibility has been proven by many of his correct actions!

We eagerly await more of these. The more Imre Nagy meets the rightful demands of the nation, the more our trust in him will grow.

UNIVERSITY STUDENT REVOLUTIONARY COMMITTEE

Page 69: Letter from Oleg Penkovsky, a senior Soviet intelligence officer, addressed to Queen Elizabeth II, the British Prime Minister, Harold Macmillan, the US President, John F. Kennedy and other senior US political figures, requesting citizenship in Britain or the US; emphasizing the need for care in Western secret services' dealings with him; and asking for money in return for his scientific intelligence.

To Her Majesty the Queen of Great Britain, Elizabeth II.
To Mr. Macmillan.
To Mr. Kennedy.
To Mr. Johnson.
To Mr. Rusk.
To Mr. MacNamara.
To Mr. Eisenhower.
To Mr. Nixon.
    TOP SECRET
To Mr. Herter.
To Mr. Heitz?
To Mr. Bracker?
To Mr. A. Dulles.

My Dear Queen,
My Dear Mr. President,
My Dear Gentlemen,

In my first letter of 19th July 1960, I have already told you that I have reappraised my place in life and about my decision and readiness to devote myself to the Cause of a struggle for a true, just and free world for humanity. For this Cause I will fight to the end.
I ask you to consider me as your soldier. Henceforth the ranks of your Armed Forces are increased by one man.
You can have no doubts about my devotion, steadfastness, selflessness and resolution in the battle for your Cause (which is also mine). You will always be satisfied with me, you will always remember me with a good word. Your acknowledgment – I will earn it. For this a great deal of time will not be necessary.
I have certain personal requests

(1) I request you to look into the question of granting me from this moment citizenship of the U.S.A. or of Great Britain. I also ask you to grant me at your discretion a military rank in the Army of the U.S.A. I have sufficient knowledge and experience and not only now but also in the future I will be able to bring you most definite benefit working in the U.S.A. itself, a prospect of which I dream a lot.

(2) I ask that you should give instructions on the careful, deliberate and conspiratorial work with me on the part of your workers.

(3) At the present moment I am handing over a series of materials which I have gathered during the last year. I ask for your directions about their assessment and about a decision on a fixed sum for this work since I have no special saving and money will be necessary in the future. I ask you to put the sum which is granted to me in an American bank.

These are my personal requests.

Once again I assure you of my boundless love and respect for you, for the American people and for all those who find themselves under your Banner. I believe in your Cause. I am ready to fulfil any of your orders. I await them.

I remain,

Always yours,

14th August 1960
9th April 1961.
See over.

Page 90:
Western propaganda booklet distributed in East Berlin describing the day-by-day build-up to 13 August 1961.

[Front cover]
Berlin: 13 August

News Flash
Berlin, 13 August (UPI). – Overnight between Saturday and Sunday, commandos of the Communist People's Police sealed off the sector borders between East and West Berlin.
UPI 6   0325   13.8.1961

9 August: A further 1,926 refugees registered in Berlin-Marienfeld.
The People's Police tightens controls in the… [text missing]

[Spread 1]
[Caption, bottom left]
An initial barbed-wire barrier on the border to the French sector.

[Text on right]
…of the Soviet sector must apply for a permit. At the same time, the number of those crossing the border fell from 12 (on 13 August it was still 13) to seven. Four of those were West Berliners, two were visitors from the German Federal Republic and one was described as a foreigner.
The Berlin Senate (West) decided not to allow the two permit checkpoints planned by the Soviet authorities to be situated on ground in West Berlin.
The Interior Minister of the Soviet-occupied zone called upon the population "to not come within 100 metres either side of the Wall dividing the capital of the GDR and West Berlin, in the

interest of their own safety". The Mayor of Berlin called this attempt to infringe upon the right to freedom of movement in West Berlin "an unparalleled effrontery".
The three mayors of the Western sectors immediately protested against these new restrictions in a statement in which the authorities in East Berlin were accused of insolence. They subsequently, under combat conditions… [text missing]

[Caption, bottom right]
The Communist regime uses the People's Police against its own people.

Page 91: Classified Stasi document showing a cross-section of the Berlin Wall and listing its specifications.

Structural and signalling reinforcement of the national border with West Berlin (at present)

[From left to right]

Primary barrier	162km
Anti-car trench	92km
Control track	165km
Column track	172km
Lighting systems	177km
Watch towers and command posts	190 installations
Anti-tank obstacles	38,000 pieces
Barrier grids	19km
Signal fence	148km
Interior wall	68km

Classified document
GVS number: G/691 880 [GVS = Classified document]
Version 1   Sheet 11
Appendix 2

Page 108: Famous edition of *Rudé Právo*, the official Czechoslovak Communist Party newspaper sympathetic to Dubček's reforms, published on the day after Soviet and other Eastern Bloc tanks rolled into Czechoslovakia.

To the whole nation of the Czechoslovak Socialist Republic
Yesterday, 20 August 1968, about 11 p.m. the troops of the Soviet Union, Polish Peoples Republic, German Democratic Republic, Hungarian Peoples Republic and Bulgarian Peoples Republic crossed the state borders of the Czechoslovak Socialist Republic. It happened unaware of *(unknown to; they did not know that it happened)* the President of the Republic, the head of the National Assembly, the Prime Minister, the First Secretary of the Central Committee of the Czechoslovak Communist Party and the institutions *(organs)* mentioned.
In these hours the Presidium of the Central Committee of the Czechoslovak Communist Party *(UV KSC)* has been sitting *(has had a session)* and dealing with the preparation for the 14th Party Congress. The Presidium of the Central Committee of the Czechoslovak Communist Party appeals to all our republic citizens to keep cool and not to resist the troops moving ahead. Therefore, neither our army, nor the Security and the Peoples Militia were

commanded to defend the country.
The Presidium of the Central Committee of the Czechoslovak Communist Party regards this act as being contradictory to all the principles of the relationships among the socialist countries and as denying the basic norms of the international law.
All the head officials of the state, the Czechoslovak Communist Party (KSC) and the National Front remain in their functions to which they were elected as the representatives of the folk and as the representatives of the members of their organizations according to laws and other rules *(norms)* valid in the Czechoslovak Socialist Republic.

Constitutional officials are immediately calling a session of the National Assembly and the republic government. The Presidium of the Central Committee of the Czechoslovak Communist Party is calling a plenum of the Central Committee of the Czechoslovak Communist Party to discuss the actual situation.

PRESIDIUM OF THE CENTRAL COMMITTEE OF THE CZECHOSLOVAK COMMUNIST PARTY

INDEX

CREDITS

The publishers would like to thank the following sources for their kind permission to reproduce the pictures in this book.

Key: t = Top, b = Bottom, c = Centre, l = Left, r = Right

Agencia Gazeta: 127

AKG-Images: 10, 20 (r), 21, 22 (t), 23 (b), 48 (t), 51 (b), 122

Alamy: DPA Picture Alliance 85 (t); /Everett Collection Historical 80 (l); /Keystone Pictures USA 12 (b); /Sputnik 73 (r); /Sueddeutsche Zeitung Photo 65 (b)

Carlton Books: 41 (tl), 42 (l), 42 (bl)

C.I.A.: 86 (t)

Conelrad Collection, USA: 44

Embassy of the Union of Soviet Socialist Republics of the United States of America: 121 (r)

English Heritage, Dover Castle: 45-47

FAS Intelligence Resource Programme: 72

German History museum, Berlin: 4, 14 (t), 24, 25, 52-53, 90

Getty Images: AFP 28, 103 (t), 112 (r), 120 (l); /Jean-Louis Atlan/Sygma 128; /Bettmann 6, 7, 9 (t), 12 (t), 16 (l), 17, 18 (l), 19, 22 (t), 27 (b), 29, 30, 31 (t), 33 (b), 34 (b), 41 (t & b), 42 (t), 49 (b), 50, 51 (t), 55 (t), 63 (bl), 64, 71 (t), 74, 76 (bl), 76 (br), 102, 105, 106 (l), 118, 129 (b), 133 (t), 133 (b), 135; /Alan Band/Keystone 77; /Régis Bossu 142 (r); /Larry Burrows/The LIFE Picture Collection 101; /Central Press 82 (l); /Corbis 40 (l), 40 (r); /Jack Esten 54 (l); /Bill Fitzpatrick/White House/The LIFE Picture Collection 138; /Benjamin E. 'Gene' Forte/CNP 59 (t); /Fox Photos 58; /Bill Gentile 134 (t), 137 (t); /Sergei Guneyev/ The LIFE Images Collection 139 (tr); /Ctsy. John Hallisey/Fbi/The LIFE Picture Collection 65 (t); /Dirck Halstead/The LIFE Images Collection 138 (l); /Hulton Archive 35, 43 (t), 100 (r), 106 (r), 107, 134 (b); /David Hume Kennerly 136; /Keystone 31 (b), 62 (l), 83, 104 (r), 112 (l), 113 (r), 123, 126 (r), 129 (t); /Mai/The LIFE Images Collection 121; /Carl Mydans/ The LIFE Picture Collection 94; /Chris Niedenthal/The LIFE Images Collection 146 (l); / Alain Nogues/Sygma 142 (l);/John Olson/The LIFE Images Collection 103 (b); /Lynn Pelham/The LIFE Images Collection 81 (t); /Piko/AFP 150; /Joel Robine/AFP 148 (b); / David Rubinger/The LIFE Images Collection 148 (tr); /Christophe Simon/AFP 145; /N. Sitnikov/Hulton Archive 9 (b); /Hulton-Deutsch Collection/Corbis 11, 13, 50 (l), 55 (b), 63 (br); /Michael Nicholson/Corbis 75; /Robert Wallis/Corbis 144; /John Sadovy/The LIFE Images Collection 55 (c); /Time Life Pictures/Department Of Defense (DOD) 113 (l); /Time Life Pictures/US Air Force/The LIFE Picture Collection 100 (l); /David Turnley/Corbis/VCG 139 (b), 143, 148 (tl), 152; /Hank Walker/The LIFE Picture Collection 36 (t)

Harry S. Truman Library, Independence, Missouri: 39

Imperial War Museums, London: 11, 20 (l), 26 (K12991), 34 (br), 69, 88-89, 104 (l), 152 (b)

John F. Kennedy Presidential Library and Museum, Boston: 87, 92, 93, 96-99

V.I.Kurenkov: 95 (b)

Library of Congress, Washington D.C. : 8 (b), 18 (r), 80 (r)

Libri Prohibiti, Prague: 108-109, 149

Mauermuseum - Museum Haus am Checkpoint Charlie, Berlin: 56-57, 126 (bl), 130-131

The National Archives, U.K.: 67 (KV2/1421), 79-79 (CAB 158/68)

National Archives and Records Administration: 6, 38, 110

National Security Archive, Washington D.C.: 14

Richard M. Nixon Presidential Materials, N.A.R.A, Washington, D.C.: 114-117

NSA: 73 (l)

Public Domain: 16 (r), 27 (t), 34 (t), 54 (r), 60 (c), 82 (r), 85 (b), 84 (l), 86 (b), 111, 133 (r)

Sergei Kudryashov: 59 (b), 60 (t), 63 (t), 124 (t)

REX/Shutterstock: 145; /AP 33 (t), 61; /Volodymyr Repik/AP 137 (b); /Sipa Press 124 (b); / Sovfoto /Universal Images Group 81 (b); /Herbert K. White/AP 31 (c); /Warner Bros/ Kobal 32

Shutterstock: 37 (b), /Mark Reinstein 152 (t)

Stasi Museum, Normannenstrasse Research and Memorial Centre, Berlin: 15 (b), 63 (br), 66 (l), 66 (r), 68, 91

State Archive of the Russian Federation, Moscow and St Petersburg, and journal Rodina, Moscow: 140-141

Topfoto.co.uk: 8 (b), 22 (b), 43 (b), 70, 71 (b), 76 (t), 125; /AP 48

U.S. Air Force: 36 (b), 95 (t), 132 (l)

U.S. Navy National Museum of Naval Aviation: 37 (t)

Viktaur via Wikimedia Commons: 84 (r)

Every effort has been made to acknowledge correctly and contact the source and/or copyright holder of each picture and Carlton Books Limited apologises for any unintentional errors or omissions, which will be corrected in future editions of this book.